Seeing Children,
Seeing God

Seeing CHiLDREN, Seeing GOD

A Practical Theology of Children and Poverty

Pamela D. Couture

ABINGDON PRESS
NASHVILLE

SEEING CHILDREN, SEEING GOD:
A PRACTICAL THEOLOGY OF CHILDREN AND POVERTY

Copyright © 2000 by Abingdon Press

This book is printed on recycled, acid-free, elemental-chlorine–free paper.

Library of Congress Cataloging-in-Publication Data

Couture, Pamela D., 1951-
    Seeing children, seeing God : a practical theology of children and poverty / Pamela D. Couture.
    p. cm.
    Includes bibliographical references (p.   ) and index.
    ISBN 0-687-08426-1 (alk. paper)
    1. Church work with poor children—United Methodist Church (U.S.) 2. Church work with poor children—United States. 3. Poor children—United States. I. Title.
    BX8347 .c68 2000
    261.8'3423'0973—dc21

                               00-026608

00 01 02 03 04 05 06 07 08 09—10 9 8 7 6 5 4 3 2 1

MANUFACTURED IN THE UNITED STATES OF AMERICA

For my children
Meredith, Shannon, and Seth

And my godchildren
Elizabeth, William, Catherine, and Sarha

ACKNOWLEDGMENTS

It seems to be part of the human condition that we spend most of our lives sorting through trivia to find that which really matters. In theological education, do we teach what students really need to know? Do we research knowledge that gives life? Do we serve within and beyond our institutions in a mutuality of friendship that brings joy? Is God and are our theological commitments permitted to shape our academic and ecclesial vocations? What if the answers to these questions break the rules we were taught, call us away from business as usual, and lead us into explorations for which we are not fully "academically" prepared?

I have had to wrestle with such painful questions in order to write this book. In the midst of that journey, I have experienced the joy of faithful companions. I am particularly grateful to the steering committee for the United Methodist Bishops' Initiative on Children and Poverty, with whom I have worked for four years. They have led me into new and important material, and steadied me on my feet: Jack and Hannah Meadors, Phyllis and Felton May, Alfred and Mackie Norris, Ken Carder, Don Ott, Elias Galvan, Emil Nacpil, Susan Morrison, Ntambo Nkulu Ntanda, Peggy Halsey, Mary Alice Gran, Gary Gunderson, Paul McCleary, Robin Ficklin-Alred, Ted Jennings, Linda Bales, Jane Hull Harvey. New colleagues in Rochester, New York, read and encouraged various portions or all of this manuscript: Bill Herzog, Werner Lemke, Richard Middleton, Darryl Trimiew, Melanie May, Linda Dolby, Paul Womack. Colleagues of many years in the Society for Pastoral Theology, in the Wesleyan Studies section of the American Academy of Religion, and at Candler School of Theology, have lent their heartfelt support: among others, Bonnie Miller-McLemore, Herbert Anderson, Han van den Blink, Don Browning, Rodney Hunter, Jim Poling, Randy Maddox, Russell Richey, Roberta and

Richard Bondi, James Fowler, John Snarey, Nancy Eiesland, Rex Matthews, Carol Newsom, Mark Sciegaj, and Mary Ann Zimmer. Good friends have suffered many discussions of these ideas: Ian and Leah Evison, Paul and Peggy Courtright, Bobbi Patterson, Cynthia Simmons, Kate Landin, Art Wells. Students, in Atlanta and Rochester, have taught me so much. This book would not exist if my editor at Abingdon Press, Ulrike Guthrie, had not encouraged it.

The Lilly Endowment funded two projects that have significantly informed this work: the Candler Congregational Studies project, under the direction of Tom Frank, and the Family, Culture, and Religion project, under the direction of Don S. Browning. To each of those directors, and to the Lilly Endowment, I express my thanks.

A special note of appreciation goes to Rev. Dr. Stephen Simmons and Rev. Dr. Robert Atkins, pastor/scholars who, at the last minute, provided advice on the final editing of the manuscript, and to Naomi Annandale, who prepared the index.

In the end, though, the book could not have been possible if the faces of my children and godchildren, and the faces of all God's children from around the world, had not reappeared in my imagination, paragraph after paragraph, page after page.

Rochester, New York
July 1999

CONTENTS

Poverty is a social, economic, and political problem of enormous proportions and complexity, and children are its most vulnerable victims. The statistics only tell part of the story: as many as forty million people die each year of poverty-related causes, of which ten million are children. Poverty threatens and sometimes destroys valued relationships and denies the world the gifts of those whose lives never reach their potential.

Compounding the tragedy of poverty's existence is the fact that it is preventable. Economic deprivation has always ravaged the earth. What is different today is that the technical means exist to prevent the premature deaths resulting from poverty. Science and technology have made available the tools for providing every person with adequate nutrition. Further, medical science knows how to prevent most childhood diseases that kill the world's impoverished children. Lacking are the moral vision, political will, and motivation to address the problems associated with poverty.

Poverty, therefore, represents a profound theological and missional crisis and challenge for the church. The God revealed in scripture is one who has special relationship with and concern for the impoverished, the vulnerable, the defenseless. Jesus announced his own mission in the images of the Jubilee tradition: "The Spirit of the Lord is upon me, because he has anointed me to bring good news to the poor. He has sent me to proclaim release to the captives" (Luke 4:18). Jesus declared that what is done to "the least of these" is done to him (Matthew 25:40).

Rarely, however, has the church moved beyond charity in addressing the challenges of the impoverished and vulnerable children. Lacking is a holistic theology and praxis that incorporates the reality of poverty and the plight of children as integral to the church's theology and practice. Dr. Pamela Couture has accepted the challenge and with this book has produced a helpful resource for theologians, pastors, and other church leaders.

As a consultant to the United Methodist Council of Bishops' Initiative on Children and Poverty, Dr. Couture has already made an enormous contribution to one denomination's understanding of poverty and the theological and missional challenges it presents. She brings to the issue a strong academic background, a deep personal commitment, and a breadth of compassion that encompasses all of God's children. This book is representative of her exceptional gifts as a scholar and pastor, and it is a gift to any church that seeks to share in God's presence with and mission to "the least of these."

Kenneth L. Carder,
Resident Bishop,
Nashville Area,
The United Methodist Church

Children, Poverty, and Pastoral Care

The central work of pastoral or congregational care is care for the most vulnerable persons in society, poor children. This work creates an ethical lens through which we can focus the general work of pastoral and practical theology. As we do the work of care and learn about the gifts, the needs, and the care of the most vulnerable children among us, we will deepen our understanding of care for less vulnerable persons and the environments in which they live. We will find new connections between caring for children and caring for families, communities, nations, the world, and the earth. We will hold ourselves accountable to a criterion of care: as long as the most vulnerable persons among us—poor children—are sacrificed as means to lesser ends, as they presently are, we have more work to do, in practice and in theory. We will also be reminded that such care is the practice of theology. Caring with vulnerable children is a means of grace, a vehicle through which God makes God's self known to us and to them. In their care we experience grace, the movement of God in our lives that allows us to give to and receive from others. We commit ourselves to love, despite the fact that no one in the world considers us or them obliged to love one another.

This mysterious meeting of God in the most vulnerable of children and in ourselves moves us to give thanks. In God we find the well of care—a deep well of living water from which flows the energy to care for the duration. Such care has deep roots—it changes lives and nourishes for a lifetime. But it also nourishes through shallower roots, roots that live among many obstacles and are more easily torn from the soil. Through deep and shallow-rooted caring, those who care with one another participate in the work of salvation. This book elaborates this vision.

Pastoral care is a work or practice of care; pastoral theology is the practical theological discipline whose job it is to conceptualize care in ministry; practical theology is a discipline that helps us to think about the work of care in relation to other practices of ministry, such as worship, and that helps us think about the practices of ministry not only in relation to the church but also in relation to the world. Each of these disciplines will be needed to demonstrate why and how pastoral care could rethink its work in relation to poor children. Furthermore, theological and biblical study will suggest some of the deep roots of such care. These disciplines are interwoven in four themes that form the chapters of this book.

Children's poverty is conditioned by two overlapping categories of poverty—material poverty and the poverty of tenuous connections. Children's flourishing is envisioned in two normative frameworks: children's social ecology and children's rights. We can map children's poverty by describing these two conditions of poverty in relation to the normative frameworks that seek children's flourishing. Such a map is necessary because engaging children and poverty as a work of pastoral care is as intellectually overwhelming as it is existentially draining.

The broad but overlapping categories of material poverty and the poverty of tenuous connections allow us to discern the different qualities of poverty that condition children's lives. The normative frameworks offer lenses through which to envision children's flourishing within a connected social ecology in which children's rights are protected. These lenses help to focus child poverty as a global problem with significantly different manifestations in industrialized countries such as the United States or Germany as compared with other parts of the world such as most African countries. In some countries around the world, especially those that are poorest, adults claim to be well connected to both their biological children and their nonbiological children but claim that social conditions, including economic policy and political instability, prevent children's adequate care. In the United States, most parents experience a natural, biological resilience that causes them to fight for their own children, but adults in the United States seem to resist sharing responsibility for one another's children, creating social disconnections that result in massive child poverty, despite general economic prosperity and political stability. The categories of material poverty and the poverty of tenuous connections and the frameworks of children's social ecology and children's rights allow us to identify the obstacles that children face and the pastoral care issues that arise in different contexts.

Children's poverty must be overcome by building relationships with vulnerable children. This work of care is a means of finding God. People in the

United States currently show a deep spiritual hunger; they seek some spiritual connection in a range of practices designed to foster that connection. Yet we rarely link the extraordinary interest in spirituality in the adult population in the United States and our problem with child poverty. So I seek to demonstrate that our potential relationships with the most vulnerable of children are also means to the spiritual connections we seek. Our relationships with poor children involve works of mercy and works of piety—traditionally called the means of grace—that, when kept in right relation with one another, give deep meaning to the love of neighbor and the love of God.

The work of care through the right relationship between mercy and piety is biblically grounded. The idea that our spiritual fullness is dependent upon our care for the most vulnerable of persons is central to the biblical witness. The Old Testament shows care for the most vulnerable person in the Hebrew community, the orphan (along with care for the widow and care for the resident alien), to be at the ethical center of mercy and piety, or care and worship. The New Testament shows Jesus to be the fulfillment of the right relation of mercy and piety. Jesus demonstrates for us how the right relation of mercy and piety is at the center of faith, the sacraments, and discipleship.

Through this work of care—by practicing the means of grace and the work of mercy and piety—the church can genuinely transform itself and influence society and culture. Such transformation depends upon the church's intimate connection with God through the means of grace and upon the church's capacity to intervene at every structural level of society and culture. Everyone can participate in the shared responsibility for this effort: individuals, small groups, congregations, and larger denominational structures. If each group in the church brings its unique gift to the table, our children will be well cared for.

FIGHTING FOR OUR CHILDREN, FIGHTING FOR ALL CHILDREN: A PROBLEM OF ADULT RESILIENCE?

Children and poverty—the stereotypical image of children and poverty is a child dying of starvation in a famine-stricken developing country. But most children living in poverty around the world—children who live without adequate food, health care, education, or parental and community support—are not the children of well-publicized disasters but children who live their lives with no media attention. They live, for example, in the bush or on the urban streets or in the homes of kind strangers in Africa, noticed by the international media only when the safety of westerners in their midst is somehow threatened. Impoverished children are also hidden in the United States—almost a quarter of children in the United States live in poverty by national standards. Those who are segregated in decaying inner-city neighborhoods have lately received much-deserved attention, but many live in rural families that have been cut off from their previous agricultural livelihood, and some live in suburban communities that refuse to acknowledge their presence.

If we imagine children independently of poverty, we too often imagine the children of middle- and upper-middle-class Sunday schools. If we imagine poverty independently of children, we too often imagine adult homeless men and single-parent mothers, as if these persons lived independently of children. All children and adolescents are exposed to factors that can deter their development, but poor children encounter multiple factors that make their lives precarious. When we think about various populations of children and how the settings of individual, community, and country poverty intersect with each other, we gain insight into the situations, meanings, and strategies of care that can produce care for all children, the adults in their lives, and local communities in which all can flourish.

Shared responsibility—these are words of judgment, consolation, and liberation. Since 23 percent of the children in the United States and many more in the countries of the southern hemisphere are poor, adults in the theological school and the church need to share the blame. We have not so ordered our lives that children may grow in love and grace, much less have their basic needs met for shelter, food, multiple stable adult relationships, medical care, and education. Nor have we organized our scholarly expertise and daily habits to solve one of the biggest problems of our time, the jeopardy in which a generation of children lives.

But these words of judgment are also words of consolation for persons who are concerned. We alone, as individuals and as the church, are only partially responsible for this situation, and we can only contribute to solving the problem. We cannot solve it alone. But we can share in partnership with others who, for whatever their religious or humanitarian motivations, want to join together to create a force that makes a positive difference with children and the environments in which they live. *Shared responsibility* become words of liberation when they result in practices that contribute to the resilience of children and those who care for them, the kind of resilience that continues to share responsibility despite overwhelming odds, gains, and disappointments, a resilience that is tenacious because it arises from God's grace.

Resilience, tenacity, and God's grace—seeing children, seeing God, surrounded by a community, we discover a mysterious, remarkable spark, a fight for a flourishing life that chastises and energizes tired adults and defies statistical odds.

The fight for survival, we know, is built into our biological self-knowledge. Several years ago, while I was canoeing with my brother and his friends in Canada, we entered a large passageway at dusk, under the waning light of a brilliant sunset. Someone noticed a shadow on the water before us—the head of a moose. The shadow passed to the shore, and the moose arose from the water, uncharacteristically transfixed, watching us, watching. Her gaze led us to look to the opposite shore from which she had come. Her calf stood, watching her. In their surprise and confusion at being overtaken by the canoe, the mother moose had continued to swim toward the opposite shore, but the calf turned around. Now, the intruding canoe threatened to separate them. The calf's gaze was riveted on its mother. In perhaps the most vivid display of emotional holding I've seen among living beings, the cow orchestrated her calf's safety. Her body rigid, fearful, strong, and firm, ready to defend in the wisest way she knew how, she resolutely turned her head toward us and then toward the calf, toward us, toward the calf. She calculated: if the calf stayed put, it might be camouflaged and out of our reach. If we threatened her calf, we would probably reach it before she did, but ultimately she would overtake us during the struggle. As she watched our every stroke for threat, her gaze held her calf on the far bank, steadying it against its impulse for proximity with its mother in the face of threat. After we passed between them, she followed us along the shore of the narrows until we paddled into the lake, then knowing that the danger had passed, plunged into the water to meet her calf.

In the moments I watched the mother, my mother's heart found hers, united by a mystical understanding of the need to defend one's young. I knew well how it felt to summon all one's psychic and bodily strength to become the first line of defense on behalf of one's children.

Such biological instinct to fight for our children can be reinforced or diminished by the social ecology in which we live. When reinforced by persons and institutions, it can become resilience. How resilient are we as a society that is willing to fight for our own children and for all children? Are we willing to join in shared responsibility with others on behalf of the long-term success of the next generation, not only in our own country but throughout the world?

At present, cultural and social energy on behalf of children abounds. In the 1990s, literature and organizations, in church and society, have heralded the plight of children. But some persons in secular humanitarian organizations and the church who have worked on behalf of children for many decades have questioned whether this explosion of popularity and energy will actually make a difference in the lives of children.[1] Skeptics in the church wonder whether the church's interest in poor children is a fad, one that the church will participate in for a few years, until we have the feeling that we have "done that" and can move on to the next "critical" issue. For children and their futures, especially for children who face an array of challenges to a successful future, short-term enthusiasm that generates shallow hope is worse than lack of interest. It creates a new round of disappointment in a group of children and their adult caretakers who know betrayal all too well. Short-term enthusiasm is neither resilience nor shared responsibility.

For large-scale, long-term change to occur, we as a society will need to convert short-term enthusiasm into long-term resilience and shared responsibility. In the midst of the immediate flurry and energy, we need to make plans for the long haul. Leaders in society and the church need to review our own small niches of the world in which we can lay the foundation for a promising future.

When the burst of energy subsides, religious faith can sustain the resilience of spirit that allows children and their caregiving friends to share responsibility for life's flourishing. We are reminded for the long haul of the words of 1 Corinthians 12:26: "If one member [of the body] suffers, all suffer together with it." As long as any children are impoverished, our local, national, and global communities—and our individual lives—are made poor also. As one more flourishes, all are enriched.

GRATITUDE: THE FOUNT OF CARE

Why make this work of care a priority? A ministry of care that fights on behalf of our children and all children springs from gratitude for life itself. Made in God's image, we received our original fight for life from God, we were received into a community of care provided by God, and we have been continually infused with God's spirit that has strengthened our resilience. We are who we are because some persons quite obvious to us—families or family surrogates—raised us. These are people we can thank. We are who we are because a whole series of people we will never be able to thank shaped and influenced us. We are who we are because people we never noticed and do not remember cared for us in a variety of ways. We may want to find creative ways to thank these persons.

Furthermore, some of us have undertaken the responsibility of raising our own children. We probably thought we would raise them entirely ourselves. But we soon discover that raising children involves a host of others—professionals, such as pediatricians and day care workers, as well as village participants, such as neighbors and Sunday school teachers. The older a child grows, the more social ecological complexity a child faces, the wider the circle expands, the more interdependent we, as parents, become with others who will share the responsibility for helping our children become the people they are meant to be. The child-rearing task is complex, as we must engage it in a world filled with sin and evil. Yet, despite all, God never gives up on us or on our children. Even when we and our children fail one another, God pronounces something within us good, made in God's image, ever ready to be transformed toward that which is divinely better than what we were.

Our gratitude can never be adequate to the gift and the givers. Rather, the only way to express our gratitude is to pass it on to others. During my child-rearing years, I was too overwhelmed to take on any additional responsibilities for children and youth. But once my own children were grown, a request in my local congregation's newsletter asking for tutors reminded me of the debt I had to repay. I became a tutor and visiting resource for children who had little family support. My first young friend was one of the unusually lucky ones; she was adopted at age fourteen. My second young friend has very little contact with her biological family. With her as my guide I have been privileged to journey to places and to meet people I would otherwise not have seen or met. She has introduced me to children who live without many of the family benefits that we normally associate with childhood. Through her I have met other children and staff who have become her surrogate but impermanent family and professionals legally responsible for her care. Together, we strengthen the environment around her otherwise fragile existence.

The life experiences of such children are an indispensable part of the hermeneutical conversation of this book, but their narratives deserve respect and care. Even though their words might move us to action, their stories deserve the confidentiality that respects each person's narrative. Therefore, I speak only in general terms about the children whose lives have touched mine in profound ways. They are among my greatest teachers. They have challenged me to see parts of myself I would rather not acknowledge. They have allowed me to become a humbled witness to their resilience. They have fed my resilience, sharing responsibility with God for transforming God's image within me, drawing me toward a good I might not previously have seen.

So, out of this sense of gratitude, I am turning to the particular niche that my work addresses, practical and pastoral theology, and pastoral care, to ask:

What difference do our children, all children, make in the way we go about our ministry of care? As a practical theologian who is particularly concerned with the practices of care and counseling in the church, the niche I am addressing in this book is that of the church's care and the theology that undergirds it, as it is taught in the seminary and practiced in the church.

WHAT DO CAREGIVERS NEED TO KNOW?

Practical theologians are in the business of practical knowing. What do practical theologians need to know to apply their existing expertise to the problem of children and poverty? Practical theologians need to know the various populations of poor children, what they have in common and how they differ, and what kinds of connections and continuities exist in the lives of poor and nonpoor children, their families, their communities, and the national and international environment in which they live. We need to know the basic concepts that guide the work of child welfare and be conversant in the language that makes the insights of the specialists' theory and research available to the practitioner. Furthermore, we need to be aware of the practices of groups in the church and in society who have exercised resilience and shared responsibility on behalf of children and poverty long before it became a popular topic. Practical theologians are potential mediators in the interchange among these groups and interpreters of the place that children, especially those with multiple obstacles in their paths toward flourishing, have within the divine-human relationship. With these voices and conversations in mind, practical theologians can contribute to strategies of action for reducing child poverty and creating a flourishing environment for all children.

The literature on children and poverty has burgeoned in the 1990s. On one hand, much of that literature has been generated by university research institutes that study child poverty, impoverished communities, and the family, such as the National Center for Children in Poverty at Columbia University (NCCP). But little university research on children studies religion or spirituality as part of the problem or the solution. On the other hand, a steady stream of literature has been generated by national and international religious leaders and church program agencies. These program materials make only the most obvious conclusions from scholarly research available to the church-going public. Scholarly research and religious interests in poverty are most integrated in analyses produced by nongovernmental organizations (NGOs), such as the United Nations International Children's Emergency Fund (UNICEF) in international children's work, and nonprofit organizations, such as the Children's Defense Fund (CDF), in the United States. Nations without strict political separation of church and state, such as the United Kingdom, have produced literature that integrates the issues that concern both church and state, especially around education and child welfare institutions.

This book draws from academic research on children and poverty, ecclesial statements and programs, NGO and nonprofit resources as they apply to children's poverty in the United States, and ecclesial traditions and theologies. Drawing these various materials into relationship with one another, this book seeks to ask why the church should care for poor children, what the theological tradition has to contribute to their resilience, and how a theology of care can help build such ministries.

CHAPTER ONE

A Map of Children's Poverties

The subject of children and poverty is as intellectually overwhelming as it is existentially draining. The details of the relation of children and poverty fly at us from the media and other sources. A map of children's poverty can bring these details into some kind of arrangement through which to organize them. My map suggests that our study of children's poverty differentiates two overlapping conditions: economic poverty and the poverty of tenuous connections. In the United States material poverty and social isolation tend to reinforce one another, but they are not necessarily coexistent: material poverty may occur among children who are richly connected to families and communities, and materially rich children may be socially isolated. In addition, leaders from poor countries report deep and enduring connections between adults and children. Social isolation is more likely to occur as individuals and families move into urban settings in search of employment. Cities provide employment, but they also separate individuals and families from their extended families, reducing the family's ability to be a safety net and exposing the immigrants to health and other risks. Therefore, it is important to consider these two qualities of poverty, material poverty and the poverty of tenuous connections, separately and in relation to one another.

My map also suggests that we think about the conditions of material poverty and the poverty of tenuous connections from two frameworks that are widely accepted: the social ecology in which children live, and children's rights. The framework of social ecology is used in much of the child welfare literature in the United States. The framework of children's rights provides internationally accepted norms for thinking about obstacles to and conditions of children's flourishing.

Children live in material poverty and the poverty of tenuous connections in a social ecology: a web of family and friends, local and national institutions, and culture. The qualities of children's social ecological nest can be described, in a simple outline, by the socioeconomic status of their families, the strength and weakness of relations with parents and other adults in social institutions, the strength of the relationships of parents and families with one another around the child, the milieu of the neighborhoods in which they live, the presence of neighborhood institutions, the government programs and services of which they are able to avail themselves, the economic forces that prevail in their communities, and the belief systems that help them make sense of their lives.

In addition, children's social ecological nest can be measured by the international standards for children's rights set forth in the Convention on the Rights of the Child, the treaty that has created more international consensus than any treaty in history.[1] The Convention protects children's civil, political, economic, social, cultural, and religious rights. It is based on the concepts of rights without distinction and discrimination, of the child's best interests, of the child's right to life, survival, and development, and of the child's right to be heard. It outlines standards for the protection of children's civil rights and freedoms, of children's basic right to live in their family environment and right to parental involvement and guidance, of children's right to receive care for basic health and welfare, of children's right to education, leisure, and recreation, and of children's right to protection in special situations such as armed conflict, conflict with the law, exploitation, or belonging to a minority or indigenous group. All countries that are members of the United Nations have ratified the Convention except the United States and Somolia. In addition to providing a widely acclaimed vision for child welfare, the Convention is legally binding on the states that have ratified it. The standards of the Convention, when understood as not only a legally binding treaty but also as an international moral code, can help us see ways in which children in the United States and in other countries may be living in material poverty or the poverty of tenuous connections.

When we use these two frameworks, social ecology and international children's rights, to qualify two overlapping conditions of poverty, the material poverty and the poverty of tenuous connections, we discover that it becomes a misnomer to speak of children's poverty. Following the lead of Michael Harrington we will more properly speak of children's pover*ties*. Harrington, whose book *The Other America* (1964) originally identified poverty in the United States as a problem concentrated in African American urban areas, proposed in *The New American Poverty* (1984) that people in the United States no longer live in poverty. Rather, people live in different kinds of poverty, the dynamics of which are unique to the region and situation in which they live. Harrington's observation is all the more true when we understand poverty in its global dimensions. Children's lives are shaped by multiple kinds of pover*ties.*[2]

MATERIAL POVERTY

When analysts in the United States calculate statistics that argue that a certain percentage of children are poor, they are usually referring to children who live in households with income below the official poverty line. Their information is based on data collected by the U.S. Census Bureau. The official poverty line in the United States was established in the 1960s by the Department of Agriculture. To create a poverty standard, the department calculated the minimum amount of money necessary to purchase a nutritionally adequate diet and multiplied by three, since families usually spent one third of their income on food. In 1996 children in households of three persons with less household income than $12,516 were officially considered poor; children in households of four persons with less household income than $16,036 were poor. According to the Children's Defense Fund, based on U.S. Department of Commerce, Bureau of the Census statistics, in 1996 13,764,000 or 19.8 percent of children under eighteen years of age lived in poor households. The young child poverty rate (ycpr) is of increasing concern: 5,333,000 or 22.7 percent of children under age six live in poverty.[3]

Some have argued that the measure of poverty should be revised. The National Center for Children in Poverty (NCCP) uses an alternative measure of income that calculates, in addition to income, food stamps, housing subsidies, school lunch benefits, income derived from the earned income tax credit, and subtracts federal, state, and payroll taxes. By that measure, 23.3 percent of young children are poor.[4]

The formula used in the United States becomes even more problematic if one seeks global comparisons of poverty. Such comparisons often begin with the per capita income of a country, based on the country's gross national product (GNP), in United States dollars. GNP is gross domestic product (GDP), or overall production of a country as measured by monetary exchange, plus and minus imports and exports. UNICEF statistics allow us to determine the wealth per capita relative to the global economy.[5] According to statistics posted April 1, 1998, the wealthiest and poorest nations as judged by per capita GNP in each of the eight UNICEF regions are:

Industrialized Nations:
$42,110 Luxembourg
($26,980 USA)
$7,910 Malta

East Asia and Pacific:
$26,730 Singapore
$220 Myanmar

Middle East and North Africa:
$17,400 United Arab Emirates
$260 Yemen

Americas and Caribbean:
$11,940 Bahamas
$250 Haiti

Central and Eastern Europe, the Commonwealth of Independent States, and the Baltics:
$8,200 Slovenia
$340 Tajikistan

East and Southern Africa:
$6,600 Seychelles
$80 Mozambique

West and Central Africa:
$3,490 Gabon
$120 Democratic Republic of Congo

South Asia:
$990 Maldives
$420 Bhutan

The per capita GNP gives some sense of a country's ability to access the global economy and provide goods and service not produced locally for its citizens, but it says nothing specific about child welfare as such. International measures of child welfare related to mortality, nutrition, safe water and sanitation, and education—data that are regularly collected and published by UNICEF—suggest standard of living conditions for children and their families. For example, we can easily compare two indicators of child welfare, infant mortality (deaths before the first birthday per 1,000 live births) and education (enrollment of boys and girls of any age in secondary school), for the same countries:

Industrialized Nations:
$42,110 Luxembourg: infant mortality: 7; secondary school enrollment: 74%
($26,980 USA): infant mortality: 8; secondary school enrollment: 97%
$7,910 Malta: infant mortality: 10; secondary school enrollment: 89%

East Asia and Pacific:
$26,730 Singapore: infant mortality: 4; total secondary enrollment: 62%
$220 Myanmar: infant mortality: 10; total secondary enrollment: 32%

Middle East and North Africa:
$17,400 United Arab Emirates: infant mortality: 15; total secondary enrollment: 78%
$260 Yemen: infant mortality: 78; total secondary enrollment: 23%

Americas and Caribbean:
$11,940 Bahamas: infant mortality: 19; total secondary enrollment: 90%
$250 Haiti: infant mortality: 94; total secondary enrollment: 22%

Central and Eastern Europe, the Commonwealth of Independent States, and the Baltics:
$8,200 Slovenia: infant mortality: 6; total secondary enrollment: 91%
$340 Tajikistan: infant mortality: 56; total secondary enrollment: 82%

East and Southern Africa:
$6,600 Seychelles: infant mortality: 15; secondary enrollment not available, but 97% reach grade 5 and adult literacy is 84%
$80 Mozambique: infant mortality: 133; secondary enrollment: 7%

West and Central Africa:
$3,490 Gabon: infant mortality: 87; secondary enrollment not available but 50% reach grade 5 and adult literacy is 63%
$120 Democratic Republic of Congo: infant mortality: 128; secondary enrollment 26%

South Asia:

$990 Maldives: infant mortality: 54; secondary enrollment 49%
$420 Bhutan: infant mortality: 90; secondary enrollment not available
but 82% reach grade 5 and adult literacy is 42%

A quick review of these data shows that the per capita GNP of a nation does not necessarily mean that its social welfare indicators will also be the highest: infant mortality in Slovenia, for example, is significantly lower than in the United States. The poorest of nations, however, have astronomically high infant mortality rates. Similarly, enrollment in secondary school is over 90 percent in the Bahamas and Slovenia, both relatively poor countries, higher than in Luxembourg, Singapore, or the United Arab Emirates—all the richest countries of their regions. While significant variation exists country by country, it is also noteworthy that the poorest of countries have consistently high child mortality rates and consistently low literacy and education rates. These countries, especially if they have been plagued by natural disaster or war, are unable to provide for the health and welfare for their citizens that much of the rest of the world takes for granted.

Furthermore, in the richest countries, children represent roughly a quarter to a third of the total population (Luxembourg, United States, Malta, Singapore, United Arab Emirates, the Bahamas, and Slovenia) but in the poorest countries nearly 40 percent to over half the population is under eighteen (Myanmar, Yemen, Haiti, Tajikistan, Seychelles, Mozambique, Gabon, Democratic Republic of the Congo, Maldives, and Bhutan). Although shorter life expectancies and higher infant mortality rates help to explain these demographic differences, these differences also hold consequences for populations. Theoretically, more adults in the richer nations are available to support the dependent and developing generation; more children in the poorer nations will need to support the family's basic needs.

When examined through the eyes of international comparisons, children in the United States should be doing quite well. In the United States, the Annie E. Casey Foundation reports that, in the nation as a whole, infant mortality has dropped from 10.6 percent in 1985 to 7.3 percent in 1996 and the percentage of teenagers sixteen to nineteen who have dropped out of secondary school has dropped from 11 percent in 1985 to 10 percent in 1996. But rates for individual states are significantly different. In 1996, the lowest infant mortality rate was 4 percent in Maine and the highest were 11 percent in Mississippi and 14.9 percent in the District of Columbia. Rates for dropping out of high school were lowest in Wisconsin at 4 percent and highest in Nevada at 17 percent.[6] The percentage of children living below the poverty line in various states also differs widely: Alaska, New Hampshire, and Utah have the lowest child poverty rates of 10 percent, and Mississippi (30 percent), New Mexico (30 percent), Louisiana (32 percent), and the District of Columbia (40 percent) have the highest rates of child poverty.

Clearly, children's well-being must be calculated by many factors. But many people ask, Is economic poverty really a factor in children's flourishing? According to the Children's Defense Fund 1998 yearbook, *The State of America's Children:*

- A baby born poor is less likely to survive to its first birthday than a baby born to an unwed mother, a high school dropout, or a mother who smoked during pregnancy.
- Poverty is a greater risk to children's overall health status than living in a single-parent family.
- Poor children face a greater risk of stunted growth, anemia, repeated years of schooling, lower test scores, and less education, as well as lower wages and lower earnings in their adult years.
- Poverty puts children at a greater risk of falling behind in school than does living in a single-parent home or being born to teenage parents.[7]

In the following bar graph, we find that poor children have higher rates of infant mortality and poorer health at birth and have more difficulty achieving in school that do nonpoor children.

It is often said that children are poor because their parents are poor. This conclusion seems obvious since the United States census statistics document the socioeconomic status of households, and much university research on poverty uses United States census data.[8] These statistics, however, do not include "invisible" groups of poor children with the most tenuous family connections: children who are homeless or live on the street, and children who live in foster homes, in group homes, or in institutions.

THE POVERTY OF TENUOUS CONNECTIONS

Families provide direct resources for children: financial support for basic needs such as shelter and clothing, access to community institutions such as schools, hospitals, and churches, and most important, attachment to primary adult caretakers who have an "enduring irrational involvement . . . in the care and joint activity with the child."[9] The poorest children in our society are

COMPARISON OF POOR AND NONPOOR CHILDREN

■ Poor

▨ Nonpoor

POOR COMPARED WITH NONPOOR

Category	Poor	Nonpoor	Comparison
Infant deaths per 1,000 live births	13.5%	8.3%	1.6 times more likely
Percentage of live births: Premature (under 37 weeks)	13.0%	7.3%	1.8 times more likely
Low birthweight	10.2%	5.5%	1.9 times more likely
Inadequate prenatal care	43.1%	15.6%	2.8 times more likely
Percentage of students in grades 3-12: Have repeated a grade	31.3%	15.4%	2.0 times more likely
Have been expelled	3.4%	1.0%	3.4 times more likely
Percentage of high school sophomores: Attended a two- or four-year college	48.3%	69.6%	One-third less likely
Earned a bachelor's degree	16.9%	32.6%	One-half as likely

Source: The Children's Defense Fund, *The State of America's Children: A Report from the Children's Defense Fund, Yearbook 1998* (CDF, 1998), p. xiii.

those with only tenuous connections to their families and communities. Homeless children often live with their families but are unable to access community services in a reliable way. Street children may have tenuous links to family and community. Children in foster and group home care receive community services but may have little or no contact with their families.

When families become homeless, they lead nomadic lives. This transitoriness may have severe consequences for the children who are still developing. As parents search for work and housing, children move from school to school or are withdrawn from school. They cannot develop a regular set of playmates. They do not receive regular, preventive medical care. Their nutrition may be inadequate. Children may have to become self-reliant at very young ages. Yet parental attachments, the mainstay of child emotional development, may be intact. Preventing the homelessness of families with children through housing subsidies and temporary assistance is one of the most important child-friendly acts in which churches and governments can engage.[10] Surrogate families that are provided through fostering, adoption, and institutional care are essential if children are to have a future.

Phyllis Kilbourn differentiates three groups of street children, according to family connection: children *on* the street, *of* the street, and *in* the street.[11] Children *on* the street, or children with regular family contact, work the streets because their families need money to survive. They are not yet deeply entrenched in street life, are most easily reached by prevention programs, and need to have family connections supported so that they do not become entrenched in street life. Children *of* the street, or children with occasional family contact, work on the street, do not go to school, and seldom go home to families. They may be from poverty-stricken families, be from deprived rural ones, have run away to escape physical or sexual abuse or parental alcoholism, or neglect and maltreatment by relatives. They need to find food and shelter daily, and a sense of identity and belonging among peers. Despite the rigors of street life, they may find the independence from adult control enticing. Kilbourn writes, "It is vital to get the children in this group off the street before they become addicted to street life."[12] The system of foster and institutional homes in the United States is designed to do exactly this. Children *in* the street have no family contact. The streets are their home. They live on the streets or in shelters, may be orphans, and may have no memory of home life. They have little ability to attach to trust, and winning their confidence is difficult.

The street children of the urban world are better known than the bush children of rural Africa. Bishop Ntambo Ntanda of the Democratic Republic of the Congo and other African bishops describe the orphaned rural children who seek refuge from war. The children fend for themselves, eating plants and living in the bush, nearly starving. They become easy prey for militia who recruit the children into guerrilla wars by offers of food.

Our images of street children typically come from the Southern Hemisphere, so we may not believe that street children live in the United States. Yet the homelessness of children is also a problem of the industrialized world, as shown by Covenant House, Inc., an international, Roman Catholic agency in ministry to street children worldwide, which serves children in New York City.[13] Furthermore, we in the United States may be shocked to find out that people come from other parts of the world to care for our street children. Tapouri, the Fourth World Movement, organized by Roman Catholics in France, sends outreach workers to the United States. Jean Claude Calliaux, a French Tapouri worker in New Orleans, in an address to the United Methodist bishops, described the goal of his work with street children in the United States, "We try to meet children on the streets, and we try to meet their parents. We listen to them, and we try to learn from them."[14]

Although the numbers of children on, of, and in the street in the United States may be less than the proportion of children in the southern hemisphere, significant continuities exist: street children are likely to be trying to escape stress, abuse, neglect, violence, and dysfunction in families or communities, but are vulnerable to an intractably exploitive world of systematized economic and sexual exploitation, drug trafficking and abuse, and prostitution.

"These children are not on the street. They are the lucky ones," a nurse told me, speaking of the children in her care. She worked in an intensive care unit for emotionally disturbed children, most of whom had no family contact or contact with the adults beyond the institution, many of whose retardation was compounded by emotional disturbance. "At least they are safe and have care." These children were receiving not only care for their basic needs, but also services, including long-term psychiatric care, provided through the state child welfare system.

According to Children's Defense Fund calculations, the number of children under eighteen in foster care in the United States increased steadily from 1990 to 1995, and in 1995 included 480,249 children.[15] However, populations of children in the foster and group home care system are diverse: many children are officially placed in the care of their extended families; some children are in permanent care of the state; others reside in foster or institutional homes for a period of time. Among these three groups of children, access to the economic, psychological, educational, physical, health, and spiritual resources of the family differ significantly. The kind of poverty children experience, whether their household is below or above the poverty line, is partially determined by the access they have to the resources of their families. It is also determined by the adequacy of services provided by their state's child welfare system.[16]

Children usually enter care of the state social service system because, as infants they are born chemically dependent, or as children they are neglected or abused. The goal of the child welfare system is "permanency planning," or providing services that stabilize a family's ability to provide care for a child without abuse or neglect; offering temporary care for a child who is to be reunited with his or her family in a matter of months; or providing a permanent family for a child through long-term foster care or adoption. The changing characteristics of children entering the child welfare system make it difficult to meet these goals. Children increasingly enter foster care with serious medical, emotional, and behavioral difficulties, such as HIV or the traumatic effects of severe sexual abuse or exposure to domestic violence.

Many children in foster care both formally (under the protection and care of the state) and informally (as a result of family responsibility and good will) reside with relatives in what is known as "kinship care." Data from the National Survey of Family and Households reveals that 10 percent of grandparents at some point assume primary responsibility for grandchildren for six months or more. Census statistics report that in 1996, 2.14 million children lived in households headed by a relative with no parent present.[17] These children may or may not live in economically poor households, but almost all experience the poverty of tenuous connection—the fragility or absence of parental support.

Institutions provide care for children around the world, and frequently, such institutions do not complement family life but substitute for families that are unwilling or unable to care for their children. For example, according to the Korean Welfare Foundation, almost all children in South Korea who are born with severe disabilities are abandoned at birth. They are cared for in the hospitals in which they were abandoned or in other institutions, including church sponsored institutions for the long-term care of children with severe disabilities.

Most poor children, however, live with at least one parent; for them, the adage that "children are poor because their parents are poor" holds true. For poor children who live with parents, whether they live with a single mother, a single father, or a two-parent working but poor couple makes a difference in the conditions that contribute to their poverty.

CHILDREN'S POOR PARENTS

In the 1980s in the United States concern developed over the "feminiza-tion of poverty," or, the extent to which mother-headed families in the United States became an increasingly large proportion of the poor. The "feminization of poverty" originally referred to an urban community phenomenon. Women and their dependent children increasingly represented the urban poor because about one-fourth of teenage males ages fifteen to nineteen were lost to inner-city communities through death and incarceration. In the late 1980s other researchers identified divorce as a primary factor causing spells of poverty among middle-class and upper-class women.[18] When one accounts for the two phenomena together, three gender-related conditions contribute to the poverty of women and children: women's wages are stretched because women are more responsible for dependent children than men; women's wages have remained consistently lower than men's wages, roughly two-thirds that of men; women are likely to be persistently poor when they live in poor communities where community institutions have declined.[19] These gender-related conditions have not changed significantly in the 1990s.

Conditions related to fathering and men, however, have changed since the early 1990s. Male unemployment continues to be a significant factor that places children in jeopardy. However, the Center for Health Statistics reports encouraging news: in 1995, gun deaths among black males decreased more than 20 percent.[20] Arrest rates among juveniles for violent crimes (murder, rape, robbery, and aggravated assault) fell more than 12 percent; juvenile homicide dropped 31 percent. This decline, over three years, was particularly strong for black children, but also dropped for white children.

Furthermore, in popular opinion and in research centers, new attention is being given to fathering.[21] In the late 1980s most publicity about fathers con-cerned "deadbeat dads" who were delinquent in child support. The 1990s publications on fathering urged fathers to become more involved, present, and responsible to the family, whether they were married to the mothers of their children or not. Even welfare reform took note of fathers. In 1996 the National Center for Children in Poverty began to "Map and Track" the states' initiatives to involve fathers in the care of their children. The NCCP recorded the various initiatives by states to involve fathers in active fathering and is tracking the development and results of these initiatives.[22]

In some circles, marriage is considered the antidote for poverty. Whereas most marriage education is focused on reducing the divorce rate among middle-class persons, some efforts focused on marriage education and parenting education are being tried in poor communities. Researchers have long thought that the lack of jobs in poor communities and the imbalance of gender due to the large numbers of men who are killed and incarcerated has deterred marriage in the inner city. As child poverty spreads to the suburbs and to rural areas, the stresses of poverty provide an additional force against happy and successful marriages. The marriage education movement may be able to assist couples to maintain marriage when poverty is working against them.

According to the 1997 "Early Childhood Poverty: A Statistical Profile (April 1997)" published by the National Center for Children in Poverty, in 1995 64 percent of poor children had at least one employed parent. In "traditional" two-parent families, in which the father is employed full time and the mother is not employed, children living in poverty grew from 6 percent in 1975 to 15 percent in 1995.

CHILDREN'S POOR NEIGHBORHOODS

Neighborhoods may be thought of as a series of systems of influence on children. Neighborhoods provide informal networks of friendship, acquaintanceship, and assistance for children and for their families. They offer formally organized institutions for support and care, such as schools, day care agencies, medical clinics, recreational organizations, and religious organizations. They become a means through which beliefs and values are communicated. Although the poverty of children is calculated according to the income of their parents, children who are both poor and not poor, according to family income, suffer the effects of neighborhood poverty.

The public has been alerted to the isolation, violence, abuse, and neglect in the lives of children in poor neighborhoods through best-sellers such as Alex Kotlowitz's *There Are No Children Here,* a story of two brothers growing up in the Henry Horner Homes in Chicago, and Jonathan Kozol's *Amazing Grace: The Lives of Children and the Conscience of a Nation,* a slice of life in the South Bronx in New York City.[24] These documentaries allow persons who are unlikely to travel to poor communities a child's view of neighborhood decline. They allow the reader to experience a child's vulnerability and resilience when industrial hygiene, police protection and fire prevention, legal businesses, medical care, and safety in housing and on the streets, fail. In the context of neighborhood social disorganization, marriages and stable family lives have little chance of success: "Nothin' works here in my neighborhood,"

35

Elizabeth says. "Keepin' a man is not the biggest problem. Keepin' from being killed is bigger. Keepin' your kids alive is bigger. If nothin' else works, why should a marriage work? I'd rather have a peaceful little life just with my kids than live with somebody who knows that he's a failure. Men like that make everyone feel rotten."[25]

Researchers have identified five neighborhood characteristics that significantly influence the social norms and individual behavior of children, youth, and parents: (1) concentration of poor, female-headed families in which supervision is lacking; (2) the absence of a middle class of high status professionals and lack of role models; (3) male joblessness that contributes to an inability to rationally plan life; (4) ethnic diversity and residential instability that erodes adult friendship networks and the neighborhood values consensus; and (5) age and gender segregation in poor neighborhoods that creates extreme child care burdens. In testing this consensus and in additional research, Greg J. Duncan and Lawrence Aber confirmed these hypotheses and added the density of housing as another feature of neighborhood disorganization.[26]

NEIGHBORHOOD ORGANIZATIONS

Neighborhoods are strong when neighborhood institutions, such as schools, medical centers, churches, libraries, and parks are thriving. Community groups are associated with these organizations. These groups provide essential formal and informal social networks in a community. These networks provide important opportunities for adults and children to interact. Adults of the neighborhoods relate to children who are not biologically theirs, and adults from outside the community, such as schoolteachers, social workers, and police, become acquainted with children. They provide supervision for youth activities. They connect youth to jobs and educational activities. Neighborhoods bring people together to solve the shared problems in a community and, in so doing, communicate the values and shared norms of a community.

In poor neighborhoods, these natural community processes break down. Residents have greater needs. So much of their energy is taken by fulfilling basic survival needs, residents may not be able to support community institutions and processes. Existing institutions and services may be overtaxed by residents' greater needs, and may have fewer resources with which to provide care. Neighborhoods may not be able to attract the kinds of persons who have the resources to sustain community involvement.[27]

The school may be the most influential institution in the life of the child, since the child spends most of his or her time away from the family at school. James Garbarino and his colleagues have described the potential role of the "school as refuge" in a violent community. The crux of Garbarino's idea of the school as refuge is "the role of caring relationships with significant adults as the principal agent of change and source of support."[28] A school that provides security in the midst of community violence is proactive in its concern for children's safety. It assumes that all children in the community are vulnerable to the multiple risk factors that lead to reduced intellectual functioning and psychological disorders such as post-traumatic stress syndrome, but it seeks to provide individualized solutions that take into account the diversity of meanings and responses that violence holds for children. As an institution, the school is designed to assist adults to respond to individual children's need for support of their resilience in the face of community circumstances they cannot control.

Neighborhoods are stronger when children and their parents know the parents of their children's friends and are involved with teachers and youth counselors. Parental relationships with their own children cannot be underestimated, but guidance from a large number of adults is optimal. "Supervision" provides not only boundaries for behavior and discipline, but guidance toward education, employment, interpreting events, and making meaning.

In a recent book *Another Day's Journey: Black Churches Confronting the American Crisis,* Robert Franklin describes his journey from being a youth in a sociologically poor community on the south side of Chicago to becoming the president of the Interdenominational Theological Seminary in Atlanta.[29] Franklin's neighborhood was fraught with vulnerability and risk, but his environment was also filled with caring adults who guided and inspired him at crucial transition points in his life. In his narrative, Franklin names eighty-four persons or categories of persons who created the environment in which he flourished. Communities with close and multiple social networks have a more secure means of guiding children through the transitions that move children toward adulthood than do communities whose social networks are disorganized.

Neighborhood institutions may support and undergird a strong family life, as in Franklin's story; they may also enrich the lives of children whose family relationships are tenuous. The Search Institute, an agency that researches the lives of children and youth, has identified a series of assets that benefits children's development. It also suggests that, although neighborhood institutions cannot be substitute families, they can effectively compensate for a lack of familial assets, so as to significantly reduce the vulnerability of a child to risky behaviors that delay development.[30]

GOVERNMENT POLICIES AND SERVICES

Government policies and services interact with neighborhood institutions but transcend them, as government creates broader policies and norms that shape certain possibilities for children's lives by creating opportunities and limitations. Government creates "family policies" that most broadly ensure child and family welfare; it targets poor and disadvantaged children in families through various welfare and social security programs; and it oversees child protective services and through child welfare agencies intervenes directly in children's lives when families are fragile or fail.[31]

In industrialized nations other than the United States and South Africa explicit family policy is developed within a framework of "universal" supports to families—that is, every family automatically receives these supports. Within this universal framework specific aspects of family policy serve targeted populations that need particular kinds of assistance. Frequently, countries have achieved a family policy that creates many programs serving a common goal because they have sought to increase or decrease their birth rates. The United States, however, has never created pronatalist or antinatalist policies, and has also not created a family policy around coordinated goals. Instead, the reverse has been true: The United States' support for children and families has been built from a series of programs and services for targeted populations that have not been coordinated by the aims of a family policy.

International comparisons among industrialized countries reveal that family policy provides three kinds of assistance: benefits, services, and support for time for parenting. Government benefits include family allowances; direct supplements to family income and/or tax benefits and reductions, child support, or a public authority that oversees the collection of and disbursement of support payments from biological and adoptive parents not in the home; housing allowances, or subsidies that make housing affordable and accessible; cash payments that provide benefits for maternity or special child related needs. Government services include child care services; infant and toddler care, and family support service for high risk children. Time for parenting is created through parental leave at the birth or adoption of a child and as needed during a child's illness or disability.[32] Until 1993, the United States did not have an explicit family policy.

Imagine the shock of a mother from the United States who moved to Great

Britain when she discovered that she would receive a weekly benefits check from the government on behalf of her children! "I don't really need this," she protested. "But you are entitled to it," she was told. In retrospect she muses, "Taxes in Great Britain were high, but when you get something tangible for it, you don't mind. The children's benefit communicated to me that children and childrearing were valued activities; that the government cared about my children, even about my foreign children!"

In the United States the Family and Medical Leave Act of 1993 began to create a framework that could put a coherent family policy in place.[33] The act deals with the issue of the universal need for time at critical points in a family's life—birth, sickness, or disability. With this act, the United States joins all other industrialized countries that have for years recognized the importance to society of time needed for a good start in child-parent relations and the particular work of the family at critical junctures. This legislation for the first time establishes a precedent that suggests that society as a whole has a stake in parental care for children at birth. The act creates the option of unpaid leave for parents who (a) work for firms that employ more than fifty at that site or within fifty miles; (b) have been employed by their current employers for at least twelve months; and (c) have worked at least 1,250 hours during the preceding twelve months. With these and other restrictions, this act requires that about 5 percent of the employers in the United States offer unpaid leave to the eligible 40 percent of the United States workforce. Individuals, however, may choose not to avail themselves of this option because they cannot afford to lose income.[34]

The United States has developed policies, and sometimes government sponsored programs, that target poor and disadvantaged children and families. Programs address such issues as poor support, education, child care, preschool and early intervention, care for children with disabilities, children's physical and mental health, child abuse and neglect, adolescent behavior that results in teenage pregnancy, chemical dependency, and juvenile delinquency, and the media.[35] The most famous and controversial of these provide support to poor children and their families: Aid for Dependent Children (now Temporary Assistance to Needy Families, or TANF), Food Stamp Program, Medicaid and Child Health, Housing Assistance, National School Lunch Program (NSLP), School Breakfast Program (SBP), Women, Infants, and Children (WIC) and other child nutrition programs, Head Start, and Tax Credits.

These and similar programs were scrutinized in anticipation of the "welfare reform" that occurred in 1996, both for their benefit to participating children and their families, and for their potential for saving future taxpayer dollars. In general, the results showed that direct income transfers to nonworking parents of the type provided by AFDC could not be proved to show direct results in children's well-being, whereas income transfers through the Earned Income Tax Credit (EITC) did. For example, children whose households received refunds from the EITC improved their housing. The results of the use of Food Stamps on behalf of children were inconclusive, but strictly targeted programs such as WIC, NSLP, and SBP improved pregnancy outcomes and child nutrition. Head Start and other early intervention programs that support children's cognitive, social, and emotional functioning produced better academic and health results.

Yet in the present climate of "moving people from welfare to work," all of these programs are considered "welfare" and even programs that have been consistently demonstrated to be highly successful, such as Head Start, are threatened.

Child welfare services are targeted at an even more select group of children with tenuous family connections. Child welfare services have been shaped by federal legislation that intersects with programs such as Medicaid to provide for children in troubled families. This legislation covers subjects such as mandated reporting of child abuse and neglect; inappropriate detention of juveniles in adult jails; identifying, testing, supplementing, and mainstreaming the education of handicapped children; the rights and governance of Native American tribes over the welfare of their children; permanency planning for children in foster care who cannot be reunited with their families; support for adolescents' transition from foster care to independent living; and creation of block grants to states for local programs.[36]

In essence, these policies reflect society's response to the multiple risk factors that are concentrated in the lives of economically poor and tenuously connected children. They mirror society's attitude toward the childhood outcomes that frequently occur as a result of those risk factors. It is generally agreed that *multiple* risk factors, rather than the *nature* of the risk factors, create the likelihood that children will become troubled teenagers who remain "outsiders" to society. In some children's lives, risk factors are concentrated. In others, one or two may exist. Every child needs a cushion against the risk factors in his or her family or neighborhood. The poorer the child, economically and in family and social connections, the greater that need.

OTHER STRUCTURAL ELEMENTS THAT TRANSCEND NEIGHBORHOODS BUT SHAPE THEM

Researchers think that certain socioeconomic trends concentrate poverty in the United States in urban neighborhoods, especially those populated by

African Americans. These large scale forces include globalization of the economy, economic restructuring (i.e., changes in the kinds of jobs that are available), migration (i.e., relocation from one place to another because jobs are available or neighborhoods are more desirable), and some public policies at the federal and state levels.[37] The influence of these forces on the lives of children and families is indirect, but significant.

Macroeconomic trends take on a life of their own; they can be more easily described and charted than controlled and directed. Despite their seeming impersonality, they are shaped by and reflect what we believe about human beings and the ways that they act. Much has been written about the belief systems that create "deserving" and "undeserving" poor women.[38] But do we have similar categories of "deserving" and "undeserving" poor children? Many researchers suggest that our attitudes toward adolescents are frequently based on assumptions that teenagers are "immature, irresponsible, and undesirable . . . closely associated in the public mind with serious social problems, among them teenage pregnancy, substance abuse, juvenile delinquency, school dropout, violence, and unemployment."[39] Mike Males, of the University of California at Irvine, has documented that despite increasing poverty rates among children in California in the last decades, socially dysfunctional behavior among children has actually decreased, while socially dysfunctional behavior (such as drug use) has increased among middle class thirty to forty-nine-year-olds. Males demonstrates that politicians, academics, and the news media readily convey the opposite impression—that the younger generation is broadly dysfunctional, while their parents are sedate.[40] But our attitudes toward the youngest children, in society and even in the church, do not communicate care and respect, according to Herbert Anderson and Susan B. Johnson.[41] Structural trends that transcend neighborhoods have an increasingly indirect yet formative influence on children's lives. Researchers such as Don Browning and Robert Heilbroner have evaluated the value structure of psychological and economic theories, finding that larger cultural and structural trends are often based on beliefs about human beings.[42] Frequently, these beliefs ignore the presence of children and adolescents as part of the human population.

ECOLOGICAL APPROACHES TO CHILDHOOD DEVELOPMENT

This map of children's poverties demonstrates how the lives of two overlapping populations of children, children whose families are economically

41

poor, and children who have tenuous connections to families and society, are nested in a series of direct and indirect influences in their environments: the social and structural ecology of children's lives. The social and structural ecology of children's lives serves as a way of envisioning an environment in which a child is well-connected and most likely to flourish.

When Urie Bronfenbrenner originally proposed the idea of social ecology, he suggested that children develop in a social ecology of four levels of systems that influence childhood development.[43] Understanding children's development within its social ecology has become a central concept in social work and public health. The systems include *microsystems,* especially families, friends, caretakers, and institutions that have direct contact with children; *mesosystems,* or interactions between the systems around the child that influence each other directly and the child indirectly; *exosystems,* or larger institutions, such as governments and businesses, that do not have direct contact with children but affect, or are affected by, children and families; and *macrosystems,* that organize and communicate broader sociocultural beliefs and values. Each of these systems impinges on the tasks of childhood development. In addition, each of these systems has both structures and processes. Structures are formal when they involve organized institutions or informal webs of friendship or acquaintanceship. Processes are the means through which neighborhood structures interact with families and children, creating the conditions in which individual development occurs. The fact of the structures, in addition to the interaction among them, builds the social and structural ecology that enriches and hampers a child's development.

Children may be seen as individuals who develop within this ecology. Childhood is understood by developmental psychologists as having multiple epochs: infancy (0-2 years), preschool (3-7 years), school age (8-10 years), younger adolescence (11-16 years), and older adolescence (17-20 years). In each of these epochs a child engages in various cognitive and social-emotional tasks, developing competencies that move the child on to the next stage. Family is the most influential structure on the child's individual development, but as the child gets older, institutions external to the family become important contexts for development. Just as children shape and are shaped by their families, families shape and are shaped by the social and structural ecologies in which they live. Children's increasing competence and strength depends on the influence of neighborhood conditions and the resources of the neighborhood.[44] Frequently, adults forget that the developmental periods of children's lives are relatively short. Five or six years of poverty in an adult life may be painful but endurable. Five or six years of poverty in the life of a child influences a third of that child's formation.

Since Bronfenbrenner's original introduction of the idea of social ecology, many researchers have modified and expanded his original concept, especially when they try to understand the socioeconomic forces that shape children's environments. We will now follow this trend, specifically asking how the idea of children's development in their social ecology is modified and expanded by the Convention on the Rights of the Child.

THE UNITED NATIONS CONVENTION ON
THE RIGHTS OF THE CHILD

The United Nations Convention on the Rights of the Child promotes a vision of a child who is well connected to his or her family, community, and nation, and their resources. A child has the fundamental right to remain connected to the multiple systems in his or her social ecological web, including families, local communities, governments, and cultural identities, that provide for the needs of the child for survival, development, and flourishing. In offering such a vision, the Convention strengthens the connections in a child's world that promote child survival and development and counteracts the intrusions into a child's life that create tenuous connections between a child and the social ecology in which a child lives. The Convention protects special populations of vulnerable children and suggests basic and restitutionary benefits that children should be able to expect from their countries. In so doing, the Convention sets out a moral vision to which countries, or "states parties," are accountable, within their resources.

CONNECTIONS BETWEEN CHILDREN
AND THEIR SOCIAL ECOLOGY

The Convention is based on the idea that children have a right to basic protection and care for their well-being, first through care from their parents and families, and then through the guardians, institutions, services, and facilities that provide for a child's well-being (Articles 3, 18). Children have a right to contact with both parents, deserve information about their parents when they are separated by detention, imprisonment, exile, deportation, or death (Article 9), and may leave and reenter any country in order to be reunited with parents (Article 10). Children shall not be denied their family identities and shall not be separated from parents, except when judicial review finds conditions such

43

as abuse and neglect that regards such separation to be in the best interests of the child (Articles 7, 8, 9). Countries that have ratified the Convention agree to respect the responsibilities, rights, and duties of parents, extended family, and community and to develop institutions that meet standards of care that provide for safety, health, and supervision of children (Articles 3, 5, 18). Countries agree to promote children's health, to reduce infant mortality, malnutrition and disease, and to educate children and parents in subjects that increase the public health of children (Article 24). In these ways, countries are specifically charged with the responsibility for supporting positive connections between children, parents, and families and for creating institutions that support parents and families in the child-rearing task.

The Convention also designates freedoms that are specifically tied to children's development: children's freedoms of self-expression (Articles 12, 13); of thought, conscience, religion, and beliefs (Article 14); of association and peaceful assembly (Articles 15, 16); and of access to media and education that provides diverse kinds of information (Article 17). In exercising such freedoms, however, children may not harm the rights and reputations of others or jeopardize national security, the public order, or public health or morals. Children shall be protected from materials that are injurious to their well-being (Article 17) and from arbitrary or unlawful interference or attacks on their privacy, family, home, correspondence, reputation, or honor (Articles 15-16).

The provisions noted above stress the varieties of ways that children's development is protected *within* family and community. These provisions do not imagine children's rights *against* family and community, except in cases where unlawful abuse or neglect occurs within the family or community. In other words, children's rights are not understood individualistically, but communally, so that countries ensure that children are anchored and protected within their families and communities.

SPECIAL POPULATIONS OF VULNERABLE CHILDREN

In support of this basic vision, the Convention seeks remedies for conditions that threaten children. The Convention seeks to prevent children from becoming disconnected from their social ecology and to protect special populations of children for whom such connections to their social ecology are dangerously severed. Countries are called to cooperate in the prevention efforts by protecting children from:

- illicit transfer and nonreturn of children abroad (Article 11).
- mental and physical violence with families and institutions (Articles 19, 20, 21, 25).
- institutionalization without review (Article 25).
- eradication of the identity and culture of indigenous or minority children (Article 30).
- economic exploitation and hazardous work (Article 32).
- sexual exploitation and sexual abuse (Article 34).
- abduction, sale, or traffic in children for any purpose (Article 35).
- torture or other cruel, inhumane, or degrading treatment or punishment, such as capital punishment or life in prison without possibility of release (Article 37).
- recruitment for armed conflict under age fifteen (Article 38).

Such provisions aim to protect children within their own countries and across international borders. Children are especially vulnerable when they become disconnected from their families and local communities, and their connection to their social ecology becomes even more fragile when that separation occurs across the boundaries of states or nations. Appeals for the care of children, families, and communities become complicated when different governing authorities are involved. The Convention creates one standard for the protection of children and the cooperation of authorities.

CHILDREN'S BENEFITS

Countries are also called upon to work together to provide for the care of children when extrafamilial or extracommunal support is required for children's flourishing. Countries are responsible for aiding children in attaining a basic standard of life and for restoring the conditions of flourishing in difficult circumstances. To satisfy basic needs countries should assist children in attaining:

- a standard of living adequate for the child's physical, mental, spiritual, moral, and social development.
- education, at all levels (Article 28).
- rest, leisure, recreation, participation in cultural life and the arts (Article 31).

In addition, countries are expected to assist children facing special obstacles:

- those who are separated from parents, by regulating adoption so that a child's original identity is maintained and by assisting children who are refugees (Articles 19, 20, 21, 22).

- those who are mentally and physically disabled, so that they have all of the opportunities for flourishing that are available for all children (Article 23).
- those who seek assistance from social security and social insurance (Article 26).
- those who seek financial support from a nonresident parent (Article 27).
- those who are victims of any form of neglect, exploitation, abuse, torture, imprisonment, or armed conflict and need care for physical and psychological recovery and social reintegration (Article 39).
- those who need access to fair legal rights and services because they are accused of a crime (Article 40).

In these ways, the United Nations Convention on the Rights of the Child sets out a vision for children's material and social ecology and seeks to create an international macrosystem that protects children against a wide range of vulnerabilities. It extends the notion of social ecology to recognize and protect those children who are most vulnerable to material and social deprivation.

THE CHURCH AND THEOLOGY AS PART OF THE SOCIAL-STRUCTURAL ECOLOGY OF POOR AND TENUOUSLY CONNECTED CHILDREN

The church can be a particularly potent force on behalf of poor and tenuously connected children because it influences society at all social and structural ecological levels. For example, congregationally sponsored preschools, Sunday schools, and youth programs are part of the microsystem of young children. Denominations also have a long history of sponsoring children's homes for tenuously connected children; usually children in a religiously sponsored children's home develop some relationships with the local congregation, so that the congregation becomes part of the child's microsystem. Congregations also sponsor Sunday schools and clubs that help adults, including parents, teachers, and social workers, develop strategies for child rearing. In so doing, congregations help parents interact with adults between microsystems, strengthening the mesosystem in which the congregation's children live. Congregations and denominations have advocacy programs on behalf of children's issues through which the church provides support for children in the exosystem that the congregation cannot directly effect. The church creates symbol and belief systems through its theological teachings. Thereby, it contributes to the theological and civil religious macrosystem that regards or disregards children.

In addition, the theological school participates in every one of these systems in that it prepares theological students, clergy and lay, to engage in practical, one-on-one ministries, to lead the congregation in its thinking on ethics and advocacy in society and culture, nationally and internationally, and to orient the congregation in the symbols and beliefs that guide its theology. Any time that the church or the theological school strengthens its contribution to these different systems in which a child develops, and any time it creates partnerships with other groups in society to do so, it strengthens its contribution to the shared responsibility that is necessary to help individual children flourish.

Bronfenbrenner argues that transformation occurs when something intervenes in all four systems that influence the child's development. Together, the church and the theological school have enormous potential to influence all four systems of which the child is a part. Too often, however, the interventions of the church and the academy, like the family policy of the United States, are piecemeal. Children's ministry is considered a minor part of the church's practical ministry, a sidebar in its ethical and advocacy thinking, and irrelevant to "correct" theological belief. Movements are afoot to coordinate our efforts and to bring the resources of the church and the theological school to bear on all four systems. In other words, the church and the theological school are poor to the extent that they are tenuously connected to the children and others in their communities who are most vulnerable, and the church and the theological school will be enriched when they are reconnected with the vulnerable—many of whom are children—in their midst.

Shared responsibility means doing what we can do to create better conditions for the flourishing of all children, particularly those in greatest need. When I say "we" in this book, I mean "the community of faith," particularly the church, the theological school, and within it, teachers and students of practical and pastoral theology and the practice of care. In particular, we are responsible for theologically specific ways of promoting the resilience of children and children's caretakers as they seek children's flourishing, especially when children live in economic poverty and in the poverty of being tenuously connected.

The problem of child poverty in the United States and internationally continues, despite many ongoing efforts by government and humanitarian and religious organizations to address it. What motivates us as religious persons not only to continue to be involved in caring for poor children, but to organize our caring efforts with poor children in our central vision? Our desire to find God, and the relationship of this motivation to the care of poor children, is the subject of chapter 2.

CHAPTER TWO

Finding God, Finding Godchildren: Caring and the Means of Grace

In a society with extensive secular social service, why does the church engage in care with poor children? Religiously based care for needy children is not the only way for society to provide, but it has the unique potential to interconnect children with caring adults through God. For two thousand years of Christian experience and many centuries of the experience of God before that, religious people have found that their search for God is intimately bound with remembering their neighbor. When they discover their most vulnerable of neighbors, Christians have found themselves and have found God. This reality is well articulated in Wesleyan theology under the topic "the means of grace." "The means of grace" is central to a Wesleyan understanding of religious experience. Caring with children and others who are afflicted, including those who suffer innocently, in the Wesleyan view, is a means of grace, a means of religious experience through which we find God.

CARING FOR CHILDREN
WHO LIVE WITH POVERTIES: FINDING NEW WAYS OF
ENGAGING IN AN ENDURING CHRISTIAN PRACTICE

Why do Christians care for children? One answer might be, "Because we have always done it that way." In the very early church, adults often "abandoned" children for whom they could not care at the door of the church—a literal "sanctuary" for children.[1] During the Middle Ages monks and nuns raised oblates, or children "donated" to the monastery. Often, parents could not care for these children in their own homes for a variety of reasons having to do with poverty or inheritance. In the late Middle Ages Christian foundling hospitals took in orphaned children in an effort to reduce infanticide. These hospitals offered a revolving door through which an adult could place a child without being observed.[2] Since the rise of modern institutions from about the 1600s, churches and their people have mentored, adopted, and fostered children, founded orphanages, created health and welfare institutions, and advocated with government on children's behalf. In so doing, churches have been involved in a variety of forms of work on behalf of children who live in economic poverty and the poverty of tenuous connections. Yet the kind of work that grounds all other effort—that instructs us in the kinds of assistance children need from adult church friends—is what we would call basic pastoral care: a one-on-one relationship with children based on respect for a child as equally worthy in the sight of God. Adults and children who care for one another in God's name are friends and companions. When friendship leads to a spiritual and moral obligation of the adult toward the child, adults and children become godparents and godchildren.

For example, with institutionalized children, such a relationship might begin with tutoring—a safe, supervised activity for which any adult who will submit to a background crime check can volunteer. A basic concept in pastoral care suggests that one cares better for an individual when one also cares for others in the individual's environment, including family and institutional staff. Just as chaplains pay attention to the needs of staff in hospitals, it is important to express genuinely friendly care and concern toward children's caregivers. If one enters a child's living environment, other children will begin to talk with a friendly visitor. It is important to get to know them as one would the friends of one's own child, making sure, though, to keep boundaries intact that establish one as the special visitor of one's own godchild. Such care might also lead to advocacy: every child in the state system needs a guardian *ad litem* who makes sure a child does not "fall through the cracks" by providing individual but nonexpert oversight through the courts for that child's care. Every child in the state system needs a mother moose to advocate for her with the institutions that provide special services.

God claims us morally and spiritually on behalf of children to whom we are biologically and nonbiologically related. In years of godparenting, my godchildren have taught me about God. They allow me to see the vulnerability of children and the spirituality that sustains them. In various encounters with them, I have truly found the image of God mirrored in their faces. Though children in our lives may be of varying material means and social connections, none are poor children but all are godchildren. It is important to recognize and describe the poverty in the lives of children so that we can do something about it. But if we label them as "poor children" we risk reinforcing deprivation as the mainstay of their identity—to them and to us. As the church, we have something else to offer: their identity is based on their having been created in the image of God. In order to remind us that all children are made in the image of God, in this book I will call them "the church's godchildren."

FINDING GODCHILDREN, FINDING GOD

The price to us may be as little as half an hour a week: for half an hour a week we can become friends who walk with children who badly need our friendship. As we do homework together, or talk with them about their aspirations and dreams, or go special places that expand their horizons, our own adult worlds grow immeasurably. In their presence we learn about vulnerability in the human condition: about tragedy, exploitation, resilience, and joy. We learn about our own naïveté, rage, and self-righteousness. We learn about the difficulty of being reliable, consistent, and faithful friends, especially when children test our resolve to be their friends. We learn about humanness, particularly when we become friends to children who are not part of our communities of comfort.

Pastoral theology has always asserted that we learn about God in the midst of humanness. As we encounter the human in the church's godchildren, in their surroundings, and in ourselves, our primary learning, if we are open to it, is about the presence of God where God is not expected to be found. In that companionship we are likely to see God's grace at work in them and in ourselves, holding us in relation, giving hope where there seems to be none, creating resilience, re-creating tragedy-torn hearts into hearts of love and forgiveness.

The church's godchildren, because they are the most vulnerable group in our society, are the ethical lens through which we need to look more closely at our relations with children and with people who are poor. In the first chapter, I mapped children's poverty as qualified by material poverty and the poverty of tenuous connections. These poverties have spiritual overtones: although providing children with material and human resources is essential, the most fundamental reconnection both for them and for us is with God.

The challenge, however, is not only imaging God in the church's godchildren but finding and living from the image of God in ourselves. Living from the image of God in ourselves provides the ground for seeing the image of God in others. Yet, it is a countercultural thing to do. It truly requires us to move to a new reality—a reality in which we acknowledge that God is already at work in our lives and in which God reigns in our lives. It is a reality that we cannot touch all of the time—but we can glimpse it and begin to live into it. The idea that we are made in the image of God suggests that we are made in love and called to live in love. This reality is our primary connection to God and to all that we do well.

FINDING GODCHILDREN THROUGH GOD: WHAT CHILDREN NEED, WHAT WE NEED

What do children need from us that arises from our sense of being made in the image of God? It has long been established that children need unconditional love—what many psychologists have called an "irrational commitment to the well-being of the child." This irrational commitment allows parents and extended family relations to transcend the irritabilities of children's lives. This irrational commitment tests adults many times over the course of a child's life but is never in doubt, providing a structure for basic trust and hope. Usually, we are irrationally committed to our few biological or adopted children. When Christians have expanded the commitment to biological children to make an irrational commitment to all children, it is often because they understand all children to have been made in the image of God. They find the face of God in the face of each child.

Children begin life fully dependent on adults for support for basic needs— shelter, clothing, health care, and other material needs. As they grow, they slowly begin to procure their own basic needs. In some settings, the transition begins early, before the age of ten; in other settings, children provide for themselves quite late, into their twenties. A gradual transition, one that involves an appropriate relation between adult responsibilities and the child's, is optimal.

Beginning with health care, then with school, then with community organizations, and finally in employment searches, children need adults among their family and friends who can connect them with community institutions. They need adults who are the conduits to the functions of caregiving, such as medical care, that were once primarily a family's responsibilities and now reside in the interdependent responsibilities of families and social institutions.

We can also be specific about the kinds of conditions in children's lives that may make their connections most tenuous. Children whose parents are immature, addicted, mentally ill, workaholic, or in severe conflict with one another may not be able to sustain unconditional love. Children whose parents are materially poor, or whose fathers or mothers are unable or unwilling to share material resources with a child who does not reside with them, may not have the basic material care they need. Children whose communities are in decline so that the social institutions around them are collapsing may not have immediate access to the institutions that care for, educate, and employ their peers in other communities.

The most serious deprivations generally occur for street children, who may fend for themselves at very early ages; homeless children, many of whom have intact families but are disconnected from community institutions such as schools at an early age; or children who live most of their lives in state custody, whose compensatory care may be provided by the state but who live with ongoing disappointments in their failure to receive the regular, unconditional love of any one adult. Our society has seemed quite willing to let children live in these deprivations, especially if we object to the lives of their parents who may be children themselves.

That children need unconditional love, care for their basic needs, and help to access community institutions seems self-evident. And yet, the lives of many children are marked by a significant deficit in one if not all of these three basics.

In the face of such a seemingly unthinkable situation, the Wesleyan belief in the grace of God—the idea that God made us in God's image, and that God continues to act in our lives—changes everything. Does this belief matter? According to James Garbarino, researcher on children who live exposed to chronic violence, it does. In international studies of children living in war zones, Garbarino and his colleagues found that children whose parents maintained a belief system and a spirituality that gave meaning to suffering fared much better psychologically than children who had no such adults in their lives. Such meaning making is significantly more likely in communities outside the United States. Within the violent sections of inner cities in the United States, Garbarino finds a spirituality present among some religious groups that buffers against chronic trauma.[3] Churches, take note! What we are doing is important, and we need to do more of it.

FINDING GOD THROUGH GODCHILDREN:
WHAT CHILDREN NEED, WHAT WE NEED

But God and children who live with poverty have a similar problem: they are not easily visible in the world. In a world that focuses on secular success,

God and children in need tend to be hidden. Both God and children are present in the world, whether we want to see them or not. But God and godchildren do not intrude on our lives. They are behind the scenes, waiting for us to discover them. They wait for us to notice that they are living in the institutions of the religious denominations to whom we contribute, working in the fields and farms as we drive by, or standing on the streets looking grown up enough to make money in a variety of illegal ways. Once we begin to notice, they wait for us while we hesitate, while we intellectualize, while we equivocate, while we work, until we hear a call into some small but regular service where godchildren and God begin to have a human, incarnate face.

We might say that godchildren are always in our peripheral vision—easy to miss or block out, but there where we can see them if we pay attention. Likewise, we might say that God is similarly in our peripheral vision. Only a very few of us are able to maintain God within our central vision all of the time. But even when we are less aware of our relationship with God, Wesleyan theology insists that God is at work in our lives. God is at work in us, preparing us to accept the grace of God in our lives. But God's grace is not irresistible—God protects our freedom to choose to respond to God's grace when and as we become prepared to do so.

The Wesleyan insistence that God has not given up on us, that God is already at work in deprived children and depraved adults, can be shocking. The idea that God's grace is already at work on the margins of our lives runs counter to the cultural ideal that we must do something—make a decision, make a commitment, act in a new way—in order for us to warrant attention or assistance from another being, human or God. At the edges of our lives, God's grace is at work, reminding us that we have already been created good. As we open ourselves to awareness, we allow ourselves to contemplate this judgment of our fundamental goodness.

The work of grace and its dawning sense of goodness also allows us to see our shortcomings, but in a different way. Grace allows us to see where we have failed children and the ideals that we thought we espoused. We see our sin more clearly. We may look back over our lives and sense sin's pervasive presence. We may feel a deep sense of failure. But because grace is doing the illumining of our sense of sin, our sense of falling short, of being alienated, or of being tainted, grace is already at work overcoming all that is sinful within us. Grace is at work for our present and our future—seeking to transform that which is sinful into that which is good. Our ability to see is also the emerging work of God in us that brings us to renewed determination. If we become convinced that we are created in the image of God and made to be transformed like God, we gain renewed determination to act godly: to act graciously as God is gracious, to love unconditionally as God loves unconditionally, to forget ourselves and our small injuries because our need for transformation into the loving and just likeness of God is greater than harboring resentments. If we believe that we are made in the image of God, we forget that we have failed and take a leap of spirit over our failures toward a life of compassion and generosity that brings true joy. We do not live from our hurt or fear that we might be taken advantage of by children or their parents, but from the presence of God in our lives.

FINDING GOD AND GODCHILDREN
THROUGH THE MEANS OF GRACE

If we begin to sense that God is active at the margins of our lives, we may begin to search for God. Sometimes, we look for God informally, simply by trying to become more aware of God's presence in our lives. Other times, we may feel the need for more formal means through which to search out God's presence and make it more vividly known. Over the centuries the church has called these more formal practices, through which people specifically seek a more intimate presence with God in their lives, the means of grace. The means of grace include works of piety, or practices oriented toward caring with God, such as praying, studying the Scriptures, fasting, singing hymns, or participating in the sacraments. The means of grace also include works of mercy, or practices oriented toward caring with other human beings, such as feeding the hungry, giving drink to the thirsty, healing the sick, visiting the imprisoned, and befriending the poor.

The means of grace is built upon a reciprocity through which God becomes visible to us and we find God. In the means of grace we find the mystery of God incarnate—God who is present in human form, Christ who is present when two or more are gathered in his name. Although works of piety seem like a more direct route to finding God, works of piety and works of mercy are mutually interdependent. True works of piety cannot exist without works of mercy, as works of mercy are the ground out of which works of piety arise. Engaging in works of mercy as a spiritual discipline—as something regularly practiced where we expect to find God—is as necessary to finding God as praying or reading Scripture. To explore this idea, we will look carefully at how John Wesley develops these classical ideas in his two sermons "On Visiting the Sick" and "On Zeal."

THE MEANS OF GRACE: A WESLEYAN
FORMULA FOR PASTORAL CARE

In his sermon "On Visiting the Sick" John Wesley develops a Wesleyan formula for pastoral care. Wesley suggests that when we engage in works of mercy, we find the kind of grace that allows genuine acts of care to occur. In contemporary language, we would say that this care is based on mutuality. As we care with others, allowing ourselves to convey God's grace to them, we are transformed. That part of our spirit that causes us to suffer or separate from other human beings and from God is made new. The mutual companionship that is offered in "visiting" becomes the center of "caring with," and leads us into a deeper understanding of our neighbor, a more profound awareness of the presence of God in our lives, and a transformed self in which we can joyously live.

Emphasizing the necessity of works of mercy, Wesley writes:

> Surely there are works of mercy, as well as works of piety, which are real means of grace. They are more especially such to those that perform them with a single eye. And those that neglect them do not receive the grace which otherwise they might. Yea, and they lose, by a continued neglect, the grace which they had received. Is it not hence that many who were once strong in faith are now weak and feeble-minded?[4]

Such an act of mercy is not replaceable by acts of piety. Rather, mercy is itself a means of grace. It is expressly commanded in Scripture, as are the sacraments, prayer, and fasting:

> "Come, ye blessed children of my Father, inherit the kingdom prepared for you from the foundation of the world. For I was hungry, and ye gave me meat, thirsty, and ye gave me drink. I was a stranger, and ye took me in; naked and ye clothed me; I was sick, and ye visited me; I was in prison, and ye came unto me." If this does not convince you that the continuance in works of mercy is necessary to salvation, consider what the Judge of all says to those on the left hand: "Depart, ye cursed, into everlasting fire, prepared for the devil and his angels. For I was hungry, and ye gave me no meat: thirsty, and ye gave me no drink: I was a stranger, and ye took me not in: naked, and ye clothed me not: sick and in prison, and ye visited me not. Inasmuch as ye have not done it unto

one of the least of these, neither have ye done it unto me." And touching this I would inquire, first, what is implied in visiting the sick? Secondly, how is it to be performed? And thirdly, by whom?[5]

Wesley explains that sending help to the sick, in essence, visiting by proxy, is not a suitable substitute for visiting face-to-face. "The word which we render 'visit' in its literal acceptation," he says, "means 'to look upon.'" It is one thing if physical infirmities prevent a person from visiting others; then, doing what good one can by proxy, such as by sending financial support, may be a means of grace. Helping from afar, however, is less likely to be a powerful means of grace if it serves the purpose of avoiding the difficult feelings that are aroused when we are in the presence of the sick, the afflicted, and the poor. Visiting from afar we rarely learn what we need to know in order to be a better human being:

> One great reason why the rich in general have so little sympathy for the poor is because they so seldom visit them. Hence it is that, according to the common observation, one part of the world does not know what the other suffers. Many of them do not know, because they do not care to know: they keep out of the way of knowing it—and then plead their voluntary ignorance as an excuse for their hardness of heart.[6]

Wesley then explains that visiting the sick, the afflicted, and the poor is an action for which no one is humanly prepared. The ability to visit comes directly from the heart that has been shaped by a relationship between the visitor and God:

> But before ever you enter upon the work you should be deeply convinced that you are by no means sufficient for it; you have neither sufficient grace, nor sufficient understanding, to perform it in the most excellent manner. And this will convince you of the necessity of applying to the Strong for strength, and of flying to the Father of lights, the Giver of every good gift, for wisdom; ever remembering, "there is a spirit in man that giveth wisdom, and an inspiration of the Holy One that giveth understanding."[7]

All of this, however, is preparation in the life of the visitor. In an actual visit the "Wesleyan formula for pastoral care" suggests that care proceeds from physical care to spiritual care to transformation of behavior. In Wesley's language, the visitor should ask first about the outward condition of the afflicted and whether there is anything the visitor can do to meet the afflicted's physical needs. Then, having shown a regard for their bodily needs, the visitor may proceed to inquire concerning their spiritual need. Only after doing these two things may the visitor teach such habits as industry and cleanliness.

In the language of contemporary pastoral theology and applied to children who live with poverty, the first task of care is to provide for the basic needs of God's children. Care for basic needs may include food, clothing, shelter, medical care, or education. Caring for physical need is real ministry and also provides the opportunity for the visitor and the visited to establish a real relationship. If this care proves to be genuine and a trust is built so that the visitor and the visited actually become genuine friends and companions, then the visitor may discuss questions of meaning and how we live in relationship with God. For a visitor to know how to discuss the meaning of a relationship with God, a visitor must be willing to learn from the visited—to apprentice himself or herself to the poor child so as to learn where and how to identify God in the relationship.[8] After a significant and genuine assistance with physical and spiritual needs, a visitor may assist the one who is afflicted to overcome self-defeating habits. In the process of learning from the visited, however, the visitor will inevitably discover his or her own self-defeating habits.

What Wesley is proposing as care flies in the face of our present culture—a culture that insists that persons demonstrate worthiness to gain assistance. It challenges the behaviorist foundations to all "therapy" or requirements for "behavior modification" through public policy that exist outside of a loving and supportive relationship. Wesleyan theology suggests that, instead, love and generosity are the fundamental relationship of neighbor to neighbor. We come in touch with a depth within our humanness when we live from generosity, and we touch others' humanness when they extend their generosity toward us. Needless to say, we hope that others will respond to our Christian generosity by receiving something from it that makes their lives better, just as they hope that we will respond by enlarging our lives because of their gifts to us. Often, such mutuality does occur.

A spirit of consistent generosity that continues even when it is not returned, however, is so unexpected that once a person begins to sense that such generosity is present, it will evoke some kind of challenge, some kind of testing. All of us have doubted love; all of us have tested it; and most of us have been the recipients of human love that survived our challenge. This human love has mediated God's love, and from it, qualities such as generosity, compassion, and empathy arise. True generosity continues even when others do not respond as we would like; otherwise, our kind actions were bait, rather than generosity. Generosity arising from the knowledge that we are created in the image of God, created to love, provides a vision of the good for us. Ideally, such generosity is simply how the followers of Jesus act. As Christians, we mold our spirits into those that can be generous even when others do not respond or when they respond with hostility, because it is good for the shaping of our own spirits to act this way. It harms us to act otherwise. But this Christian behavior may have its most powerful influence on others when it persists, but does not insist on its way, in adverse circumstances.

PASTORAL CARE, SPIRITUAL FORMATION, AND WORSHIP

The work of mercy offers a connection with God that is vivid but indirect—it is mediated through our experience with another human being or with a community. In contrast, the work of piety is direct—it is focused upon our relationship with God. The history of humankind shows that once we feel connected to God, humans have a tendency to skip the work of mercy and proceed directly to the work of piety in order to experience a direct relationship with God. Then, we begin to think that the work of piety, directly focused on God, is more important than the work of mercy. Yet the indirect experience of God through mercy is an essential part of the experience of grace.

In his sermon "On Zeal" Wesley offers guidance to those who would be tempted to shortcircuit mercy because they think that piety is more important. Works of piety and works of mercy are equally important, but when they conflict, works of mercy have priority. In his sermon "On Zeal" Wesley writes that Christians should show zeal for works of piety, but much more for works of mercy:

> Whenever, therefore, one interferes with the other, works of mercy are to be preferred. Even reading, hearing, prayer, are to be omitted, or to be postponed, at "charity's almighty call"—when we are called to relieve the distress of our neighbour, whether in body or in soul.[9]

Our work of mercy deepens our work of piety. The connectional tissue between the work of piety and the work of mercy is God's grace. God becomes most visible and vivid to the world when the work of mercy and the work of piety are organically related to one another.[10]

When we practice the means of grace and seek the revelation of God in our works of mercy, religious experience is heightened as a means of intimacy with God. God is revealed. When such reconnection occurs, it brings vitality to personal devotions and public worship. Life becomes more vivid. We recognize sin and evil more fully but we can sustain our connection to God, even when we become aware of sin. We experience grace more fully as an experience that provides an alternative way of living. The energy that can feed anger or hostility can be reshaped into love. We may actually begin to sense what Jesus might have meant when he said that an alternative reality of God's reign is with us—now.

PASTORAL CARE AND REVELATION

If through the work of mercy we discover that God's reign is at hand, then pastoral care as a means of grace—pastoral care as the work of mercy that becomes the ground for the work of piety—is directly related to the revelation of God in the world. How does God become known to us? Very simply, we know God because God reveals Godself to us. Scholars have argued for centuries over how God reveals. Has God revealed Godself once and for all in a deposit of writings—Scripture or church writings—that we call revelation? Yes, God has revealed Godself, but no, not once and for all. Revelation as a noun is a dead relic without its verb form, "to reveal." In the passive form of the verb, God "is revealed," I can ask significant questions about my pastoral work: in the course of my writing or my teaching or my caring relationships with godchildren, is God revealed? Or, should I say, do I hope that God is revealed? Yes, I do. In the active form of the verb, however, I can be even more theologically precise and true to Wesleyan tradition: God reveals. God does God's own revealing. The question becomes: in the course of my writing or teaching or pastoral work does God reveal Godself? If *God reveals,* the fact that I have invoked "God" does not mean that God is revealed. Nor does the fact that I have not invoked "God" mean that God has not been revealed.

Only after affirming the active verb form, God reveals, and the passive form, God is revealed, does the noun, revelation, become a living concept. The deposits of revelation—Scripture and tradition—must be actively illumined by God's grace in our reading and hearing for revelation to occur. Only then do the deposits of revelation make possible the kind of connection between God and humanity that allow us to experience God's revealing.[11]

Wesleyan theology has a strong doctrine of prevenient grace. Prevenient grace is the activity of God in our lives that precedes our knowledge of God, the grace that I referred to earlier as being in our peripheral vision. Scripture, tradition, reason, and religious experience aid the action of God's grace.[12]

Through prevenient grace God is always reaching toward us, inviting us into relationship with divine personhood and with the rest of humanity. Through prevenient grace God also prepares us to extend ourselves toward God, even though God leaves it up to us eventually to move toward God.

In Wesleyan language, God is quickening our spiritual senses, opening us to the possibility of religious experience. Although that language is archaic and arises from an epistemology of the eighteenth century, it may be a way of talking about an elusive experience of God in pastoral care.[13] We have few words through which to describe that mystery in pastoral work that occurs when our insight is deepened, our spirits are moved, and we sense a new openness in ourselves and others to something previously unknown, something that points beyond ourselves. The metaphor of the quickening of the spiritual senses helps to describe that experience. The metaphor reminds us of a reality that grounds pastoral care for which our language is thin. God has already been and is constantly working within us—working to deepen our self-awareness in order to make us whole in the image of God.

In very simple terms, we care for godchildren in response to God's work in our lives, and we strive to create the conditions in which God reveals God-self.

THE WORK OF MERCY REVEALS OUR GOODNESS, OUR SINFULNESS, AND GENUINE EVIL

In pastoral care, when our spiritual senses are quickened, we recognize not only goodness, but also sin and evil. People may resist doing the work of mercy with the church's godchildren, in part, because it arouses in them feelings they would rather not have, often related to their experience of sin and evil, or confronts them with life situations they would rather not know exist. These experiences may be related to deprivation, violence, loss, exploitation, shame, or guilt. Although training in pastoral care and counseling tries to help people become present to the experiences of goodness, sin, and evil in a measured way, the general work of mercy in the church opens our eyes to that which we would rather not see: in ourselves, in others, in the church, and in society. The work of mercy takes us where we may not have gone before and where we may not yet be prepared to go. In the words of the book of John: "Jesus said to him, 'Feed my sheep. Very truly, I tell you, when you were younger, you used to fasten your own belt and to go wherever you wished. But when you grow old, you will stretch out your hands, and someone else will fasten a belt around you and take you where you do not wish to go'" (John 21:17-18).

Pastoral counseling teaches that a counselor can only go as deeply into human experience with a counselee as the counselor has gone. Yet in pastoral counseling training it is often the counselee's experience that nudges the counselor to enter more deeply into his or her and the counselee's own experience. So it is with the work of mercy: the work of mercy inevitably takes us deeper into human experience. As in counseling, this walk can be measured. Fundamental to the work of mercy, especially with children, is this: Do not rush to save the world. Begin small. Consider commitments carefully. Make only the commitments you can keep. Do not underestimate the accumulating value of small, regular commitments. Reflect on your experience; pray about it; learn from it; walk with God in it. Anticipate that you will find new and disturbing forms of sin and evil, but that you will also find grace.

The experience of sin, evil, and depravity, and the experience of grace are both religious experiences. Theologically and mythologically, the language of sin provides a word through which we can speak of the experience, in ourselves and in others, of inevitable and universal shortsightedness, failure, alienation, and malice. The language of evil provides a way of speaking of the interlocking systems at every level of our social structure that provide inordinate privileges for some people and obscure the exploitation of others. Systemic evil characteristically depersonalizes privilege and exploitation, and the system is so far removed from the control of persons that systemic relations become invisible. The language of depravity helps us acknowledge that we cannot remove ourselves from sin, or even extract ourselves from evil relations. All of us participate to some extent in the exploitation of others. In contrast to our culture that tells us that we have choices about everything and that we are responsible for all of our choices, the language of sin, evil, and depravity tells us that we will inevitably be entangled in relations that do not live up to the example that God, through Jesus, has offered to us. One of the most wicked signs of the reality of sin, evil, and depravity is that godchildren are so often at the vulnerable end of the chain of exploitation.

As we do the work of mercy, our experience of sin, depravity, or evil in the world intensifies. We may find ourselves mentally paralyzed or enraged, but unable to act. Simultaneously, sin, depravity, and evil lose their power over us as we look back on it through the illumination of grace. God's grace allows us to recognize the personal sin, systemic evil, and depravity that we experience in ourselves and in the world. As God helps us recognize sin and evil, even the fact of our recognition shows us that God's grace is already at work in us.

God's grace is available to open our hearts to justifying grace—a grace that restrains us from wallowing in our own or other's sin by opening us to God's forgiveness and acceptance and the possibility of God's renewing God's image in us and in the world. When we recognize that such transformation is at work, we are prevented from using the knowledge of sin and evil as a whip against ourselves or others.

THE HAN OF GODCHILDREN

Godchildren sometimes suffer, often intensely, and behavioral problems result from this suffering. A theology of children and poverty faces the complicated task of describing, without minimizing, the agony that many children bear and the behavioral problems that become symptoms of that agony. The traditional language of sin, evil, and depravity does not allow us adequately to articulate the problem. Our most tenuously connected children are innocent victims; much of their problematic behavior arises from their victimization; yet for the possibility of their own futures, their overwhelming suffering must be relieved as they are simultaneously guided to control their behavior. Many of their parents are children themselves, also innocent victims. The children and the caregivers engaged in this endeavor deserve respect, spiritual support, and a theology adequate to their task.

The concept of han from Korean minjung theology offers helpful distinctions that augment our traditional language of sin, evil, and depravity. Han refers to the suffering that is accumulated in the victims of sin, burdening them with agony. For our purposes, han describes the "abysmal experience of pain," of the child, for example, who is abused, neglected, or sexually exploited; who is torn from friends, family, and school by homelessness; who is separated from her parent because of the parent's incarceration at a distance; who watches his parent deteriorate from alcohol or drug use; whose sibling or close friend is killed in meaningless violence; who is hungry or sick with inadequate care. Han focuses on the pain of the victims and reserves the language of sin for willful acts that victimize others.[14]

Han, according to Andrew Park, author of *The Wounded Heart of God: The Asian Concept of Han and the Christian Doctrine of Sin,* has a specific structure. It manifests itself passively and actively, consciously and unconsciously. The passive, unconscious han implodes into despair, helplessness, and hopelessness. The active, unconscious han results in bitterness. Passive, conscious han accumulates in the sense of self of people who have been oppressed over a long period of time and whose sense of hope has been destroyed. Active, conscious han results in the collective will to revolt, and it arises when "public wrath and rage respond to any oppressive public policies and unjust work."[15] At the bottom of han is the deeply wounded heart, the kind that is often best expressed in poetry such as that of Sung Woo Yang:

> Curse, curse, you mountains, rivers, trees, and grass! cry, beating your breast; because you will be able to live billions of years; To curse the offspring of the offspring of those who bear swords. . . .[16]

HAN AS DESCRIBED IN THE BOOK OF JOB

To imagine the difficulty that Christian theology has had in dealing with han, think of the biblical book of Job and the sermons that you may have heard (or preached) on it. Many of our interpretations of Job are attempts to relieve prematurely our own anxiety about the han it describes. Job, a formerly wealthy man, is not at fault for his agony. To resolve an argument between God and Satan over the extent of his righteousness, his achievements, comforts, and even his health are ripped from him, without his knowing why. In the story, Job's friends (and many preachers) cannot enter fully into his experience. They think that Job's suffering is so extreme that he must have done something to deserve his suffering. If not, their meaningful universe will fall apart. As readers of the story, we distance ourselves from the possibility that this could happen to us by accepting the friends' assignment of blame. Or we get entangled in debates over what the beginning of the story says about the nature of God: how can we imagine God playing with humanity in such an irresponsible way? Or we jump too quickly to the conclusion of the book of Job, in which Job and God are reconciled: Job is to blame because he is being "impatient" with the ways of God. When we leap to these conclusions, we distance ourselves from the possibility of undeserved suffering by assigning blame. We lose the opportunity to experience han in one of its most powerful biblical descriptions.

If we enter the text empathically with Job, imagining ourselves in his place, we confront the horror of his life and find Job working his way through the structure of han of which Park speaks.

Hearing of his distress, Job's friends come to comfort him. They are shocked by the severity of his suffering and wait silently at his side, as good friends would, until Job is ready to speak. For days, they sit with Job in his passive han. Once his han becomes active, they find it very difficult to befriend him.

After seven days and seven nights of silence, Job's bitterness explodes. Job's friends offer only the most superficial empathy for his situation, as they are secure in their assumptions that good behavior will always be rewarded and that Job must be to blame. Job's friends challenge Job's attempt to justify his bitterness against God in increasingly harsh language. This peace is broken by rancor when Job will no longer accept their simple answer: If Job is suffering, then he must have done something terrible to deserve his fate.

In order to make his friends realize how cruel their words sound in the midst of his distress, Job appeals to his friends to have sympathy for his plight, using a vivid image for their cruelty: "You would even cast lots over the orphan, and bargain over your friend" (Job 6:27). Instead, the friends become increasingly harsh. One of Job's friends, Eliphaz the Temanite, challenges Job's belief that he is righteous by accusing Job of exploiting widows and orphans: "You have sent widows away empty-handed, and the arms of orphans you have crushed" (Job 22:9). These words show the intensity of their disagreement, as Job and his friends agree that it is the height of insult to be accused of exploiting the widow and the orphan.

This insult is likewise hurled toward God. Job is angry that God does not intervene in suffering, and instead leaves the vulnerable in agony. God is an absent God who will not judge between disputants, who leaves the vulnerable to their fate, while allowing the unjust to reap the rewards of their exploits:

> "Why are times not kept by the Almighty,
>   and why do those who know him never see his days? . . .
> They drive away the donkey of the orphan;
>   they take the widow's ox for a pledge. . . .
> There are those who snatch the orphan child from the breast,
>   and take as a pledge the infant of the poor. . . . .
> They harm the childless woman,
>   and do no good to the widow.
> Yet God prolongs the life of the mighty by his power;
>   they rise up when they despair of life. . . .
> If it is not so, who will prove me a liar,
>   and show that there is nothing in what I say?" (Job 24:1-25)

The problem we are shown is that in order to become transformed, innocent suffering strikes back, confusing us and destroying any romanticization of what it means to journey with those burdened with han.

After intense emotional struggle with God and his friends, Job's active han begins to abate. In chapter 29: 2, 5, 12, Job's rage gives way to lament, as he stands before God grieving for what he has lost—his family, his possessions, and his well-deserved honor as a just man who protected the vulnerable, including the orphan:

> "Oh, that I were as in the months of old,
>   as in the days when God watched over me;
> When the Almighty was still with me,
>   when my children were around me;
> because I delivered the poor who cried,
>   and the orphan who had no helper."

In the conclusion of the book, Job's righteousness is vindicated and Job "resolves" his han in the mystery of God (Job 42:1-6). This resolution is taken a step further by the "epilogue" when God urges the friends to seek Job's forgiveness, and Job prays for them (Job 42:7-10). Job's fortunes are restored, but this conclusion need not domesticate or trivialize the extreme suffering that the poetry of the book of Job communicates. Ironically, acts of mercy that bring us face-to-face with innocent suffering are perhaps the hardest befriending to which we are called. Job's friends were far more present to innocent suffering than most of the rest of us; they walked through the hell of that suffering with him, even though they were not able to stay present and empathic with it; and they could be reconciled with Job as friends in the presence of God at the end of their journey together. Job's friends let us know that, in the beginning, we will set out to care for those who suffer, but at the end of the journey, we will probably need to seek their forgiveness. The question is whether it is better to befriend, fall short, and return to befriending, than never to befriend at all.

Might we, for the sake of mercy, be willing to embark on a similar journey? Might we use the biblical text to instruct us in what it means to sit in the presence of extreme suffering, whether that suffering is found in a biblical text or in a child? Might we take the relationship between Job and his friends as a reality check? Might we hold out a vision of being present to innocent suffering without intellectualizing, blaming, distancing, protecting ourselves, or prematurely pushing toward resolution, but also of having self-awareness when we fall short, knowing that such defensiveness will occasionally occur? The book of Job is, to my mind, an excellent biblical example of narrative pastoral theology and an opportunity to prepare ourselves to enter into suffering with others.

THE TRANSMISSION OF HAN

Park uses the example of children to discuss the fourfold transmission of the structure of han. In our need to assign blame, children have often been considered sinful as a result of original sin, often with the resulting consequence that their sin must be stricken from them by physical discipline. The idea of han avoids this understanding. First, han may be transmitted biologically. For example, a child who inherits the genes for a disease inherits not his parent's han, but "the seat of han." Second, a child is bequeathed his parent's mental and spiritual han. A child will probably take on his parent's deep-seated parental melancholy, bitterness, and resentment without even being aware of it. Third, a child may receive han in the social environments in which he lives. The child may be shaped by the effects of patriarchy, hierarchy, racism, ethnic conflict, or violent lifestyles. Fourth, a child is bequeathed racial han and the historical traumas inflicted upon some races.

Park points out that the doctrine of original sin tries to portray the "solidarity of the human race" but needs to be met with "'original han,' which is caused by the unfair transmission of the first parents' sinful nature. The idea of han may be a way to save and preserve the doctrine of original sin, whose principal intent is to describe the deep and connected dimension of the human predicament."[17] Without a concept like han, pastoral theology has been in a quandary. It has depended on psychology to "understand" that human behavior often originates in deep-seated traumas, and in doing so has been ill equipped to articulate ways to distinguish responsibility for behavior resulting from extreme pain. Because of this lack, the "theology" surrounding these circumstances is more likely to be created in the child's unit of the hospital or in juvenile court than in the classroom of the school of theology or in the church.

Park writes that han is resolved when it meets understanding, hope, engagement in action, and compassionate confrontation. For a child, this resolution will transform the tragic behavior that results in violence against self or others into a positive, gentle sense of self, optimism toward the future, and well-channeled or even constructive use of anger. A child who is able to resolve her han is able to share in responsibility for her future.

A remarkable story of an adult's resolution of the han of chronic depression is told by Tracy Thompson in *The Beast: A Reckoning with Depression.* Persons with chronic depression resonate with the book; persons who have not experienced depression may find new levels of understanding of the tentacles of depression that reach into the soul to distort, immobilize, and paralyze. After telling a story of years of living with behaviors and their consequences that spoke of a depression too deep for words, Thompson describes her early search for a language for depression. Psychobabble fails to touch her struggle to resolve her suffering. She discards such concepts as "tough love . . . an idea that appeals, more strongly to the persons applying the discipline that those receiving it." She turns away from media messages that communicate "whatever happens, whatever you've done, don't think ill of yourself," and shrinks from office seminars that emphasize positive thinking. These languages did not adequately understand the depth of her suffering, the expanse of her han. They were, like Job's friends, short of the mark of understanding. Nor did they help her gain a realistic assessment of herself so that she could move on to a compassionate confrontation with herself and others. Eventually the words came:

> Now at long last, I realized: it was both—both loving myself, and putting myself out there to be judged in the eyes of others. If I loved myself, I could learn to forgive my mistakes. And yet as long as my self-esteem relied in some part on what other people thought of me, I would be motivated to try for tangible accomplishments—a far sturdier foundation for my self-regard than empty ego puffery or "I feel good about myself" psychobabble.
>
> The trick was unsparing, unsentimental honesty. There were bad things in view when I looked in the mirror; my job was to figure out what they were, to see them in proportion, and not to flinch. "No Whining Allowed." The button was stuck on the bulletin board above my desk at work as a silent reminder: touch self-love. Learning how to love myself had given me a reason to survive a debilitating and terrifying episode of depression; it was the rope I had hung on to in the pit of despair. But being tough on myself was the pulley. It was the thing that got me out.[18]

Can a child's han be resolved by such a sophisticated conclusion? One would think such self-understanding to be far beyond the meaning that a child could attach to her life. Yet my visits to children's homes and therapeutic centers for severely traumatized children suggest just that. The children's successful future is dependent upon a goal of the present—creating an environment of deep empathy, as deep as God's ultimate compassion for Job, and structure within which the child can take responsibility for his or her life. Usually, this process is not linear and involves periods of progress and backsliding. As genuine, age-appropriate responsibility develops and is supported, the child will be able to function well in the institutions of her care. Eventually, the child may be able to go another step to transform his or her deep wounds into the power of good for others.

Church care recognizes suffering, and it supports and affirms responsibility. But religiously based care goes a step further and places all human experience within the grace of God. Religious experience opens us not only to health, but to renewal in God's image. When Wesley emphasizes this idea, Randy Maddox argues, he draws upon the therapeutic imagery of the Eastern church fathers. For the early Roman church, we come before God as if in a courtroom—forensic metaphors of forgiveness dominate the understanding of the action of grace. And Wesleyan theology certainly adopts this understanding. But for all the good it does, forgiveness only resolves guilt. It does not also heal the trauma for which we are not to blame. To heal trauma, to identify with innocent suffering, theology needs a language of God's healing that does not only depend on forgiving guilt. Wesleyan theology has such a language, one taken from the therapeutic metaphors of the Eastern church. While the minjung concept of han describes the human experience of innocent suffering, the Wesleyan idea that God's grace comes to us in order to renew the image of God in humankind is an antidote to such suffering.[19] This therapeutic emphasis in Wesleyan theology makes it a deeply pastoral theology, one whose vision of healing resonates with the clinical therapeutic tradition of the twentieth century. If God is present as we become self-aware, godchildren and we can be freed from reactions that arise from the denial of guilt and shame, and godchildren and we can be freed from the suffering into which inordinate guilt and shame lock us. Godchildren and we may not be free from the seat of han, but in the presence of others may be freed from allowing han to determine the outcome of life. God can transform both ordinate and inordinate guilt and shame into the light of God that allows our lives to reflect God's image to those around us.

JOB AND HIS FRIENDS AND THE MUTUALITY OF MERCY

Despite the failures of empathy in their relationship, the deep mutuality of mercy that exists in relations among people who care for one another is evident between Job and his friends; that mutuality of mercy is also evident in the dynamic relation of self-with-self in the evolution of self-care of Tracy Thompson. This relationship of mutuality and interdependence is also evident between mercy and piety in their private and public manifestations.

Initially, a power imbalance exists between those cared for and those in need; a power imbalance may also exist between our caring and our needy parts of ourselves. Within a short time, people who enter deep relations, with others and with themselves, discover that acts of mercy continually reorganize that power relationship, until people who share in acts of mercy give to and receive from one another.[20] This reconstruction of power relations is the work of grace. It points toward what theologian Jon Sobrino has called living by "the principle of mercy"—acting with mercy whenever one is in the presence of suffering, only because suffering exists.[21] It prevents what it classically understood as "the work of mercy" from degenerating into what is perjoratively known as "charity." Mercy and charity in their older, theological sense, do not refer to the kind of paternalistic, dependence-creating, client relations that we associate with contemporary, secularized understandings of mercy and charity. Acts of mercy and charity, in their Wesleyan sense, reshape the Christian character and the spirits of all participants.[22]

Mercy as used here is predominantly private and interpersonal—the domain of pastoral care—but leads, through the work of grace, to public acts. In Sobrino's words, the work of mercy "consists in making someone else's pain our very own and allowing that pain to move us to respond."[23] Once mercy quickens the spiritual senses, opening a person to grace, sin, and evil, and calling a person to enter into a han-like journey, part of the resolution of that han and the transformation of grace seeks its expression in public form: in relation to God in worship, and in relation to other human beings in justice. In other words, acts of mercy and acts of personal piety, such as personal prayer and individual Scripture reading, find their *telos,* or aim, in publicness—in worship and in justice. Mercy, personal piety, public worship, and justice are integrally related to one another. Acts of mercy provide trust and hope through interpersonal presence. Then, we take what we have learned from God into the various arenas where that knowledge needs to influence the world. When learning occurs in the interpersonal realm that suggests that trust and hope must also be built through public acts, mercy is incomplete until it has found its home in justice.

Mercy, personal piety, justice, and worship are too often separated from one another by those who would emphasize either interpersonal relations or social transformation. The story is often repeated of the person who does individual acts of mercy, rescuing bleeding bodies from the river, and eventually walks upstream to find out why so many bleeding bodies are floating downstream. The implication is that if the situation can be righted at its source, there will be no more bleeding bodies. While radical transformation, or change, at the root of a problem is a necessary act of justice, it is also essential that we not allow bodies and souls to bleed to death while we wait for justice to be done.

69

This is especially true when we are speaking of the bodies and souls of children in their formative years. We also should not assume that any social transformation will be perfect, and once social transformation occurs, no one will bleed. Mercy calls us to attend to all that is before us, for the sake of those who are bleeding, for our own sake, and in the imitation of Christ. Deep mercy, the kind that can lead to justice, will always be required. Such mercy is so powerful that it transforms our piety and worship.

Why does the church care for godchildren? Caring for godchildren, entering into their experience, is the deepest kind of friendship that is possible, one that invites the mutuality of power rearrangements and is inextricably bound to our experience of God. Such religious experience has private and public manifestations. One of the most public witnesses to this experience of God and humanity is in Scripture. In the next chapter we find that the deep interrelationship of the work of mercy and work of piety is at the center of the biblical portrayal of the relationship of God and humanity. In the Old Testament we learn that a close relationship of mercy and piety, in private and public expressions, is central to what it means to care. In the New Testament we see that Jesus Christ is the example and fulfillment of what it means to care.

CHAPTER THREE

Mercy, Piety, and Care
in the Christian Bible

THE OLD TESTAMENT: THE CENTRALITY OF
THE RIGHT RELATION BETWEEN MERCY, PIETY,
CARE, AND GODCHILDREN[1]

The Old Testament is fraught with both agony and vision. Reading it as a pastoral theologian, I am struck with the words it speaks to the concerns about "spirituality" that are so prevalent in our time. In a country of such accomplishment as the United States, why is our society so worried about spirituality? Is our concern about spirituality a sign that we find ourselves not only alienated from ourselves and inaccessible to our family, friends, and neighbors, but also unwilling to invite the orphan, the widow, the resident alien, and equivalently needy persons into worship and church life, in addition to being unwilling to meet their physical needs? Could it be that a profound movement of the spirit, from which we are encouraged to drink, can be found in a few basics from the law, the poets, and the prophets: seeing anew the widow, the orphan, the resident alien, and all others who are vulnerable, finding God in the practice of mercy, justice, and righteousness, and giving thanks for the God we find in our neighbor? Is this spirit not the source of all pastoral care?

THE ORPHAN AS THE VULNERABLE AND POOR CHILD
IN THE OLD TESTAMENT

In the Old Testament the poorest of poor children is "the orphan." The orphan figures centrally into the Old Testament teachings about the gracious nature of God and the anticipation that the religious community will reflect God's nature in its mercy and its piety. Yet biblical commentaries of the kind that pastors and laity are most likely to use to guide their study of the Bible reflect our society's tendency to dissociate children and poverty.[2] Extensive biblical commentary exists on the role of the poor in the Old and New Testaments.[3] For example, the *Anchor Bible Dictionary* entry on "The Poor" explores the role of different categories of people, all of whom are rendered "the poor" in the English translation of the Old Testament: small farmers, day laborers, construction workers, beggars, debt slaves, and village dwellers.[4] The poor in the New Testament are identified not as categories of people but by the manifestations of their poverty: they are hungry, thirsty, naked, homeless, unemployed, dispersed from their homes.[5] But specific mention of children as a group of vulnerable persons among the poor is minimal.[6] Little commentary exists on the role of children, poor or otherwise.[7] Even so, poor children exist as important players in the biblical drama when we seek to do biblical theology or ethics.

GOD AS THE PROTECTOR OF THE DESTITUTE

Most people of faith would argue that the Ten Commandments form the ethical center of the Old Testament. The inextricable relationship between mercy and piety is found in the first commandment of the Decalogue: "I am the LORD your God, who brought you out of the land of Egypt, out of the house of slavery; you shall have no other gods before me" (Deuteronomy 5:6-7).

Piety, here, refers not to a specific expression of piety, such as prayer, Scripture reading, and fasting, but to the loyalty and gratitude that grounds any specific practice of piety. Here, all piety, public and private, is centered in the community's remembering that God provided the exodus and, therefore, is the God toward whom the Israelites owe their ultimate loyalty. But this appeal for the community's piety is directly related to the fact of God's mercy in bringing the Israelites out of slavery in Egypt. The biblical writers do not exhort the specific care of the widow, the orphan, and the alien until later writings that are commentary on the Decalogue. But when the writers tell the community to care for the widow, orphan, and alien, the community is frequently reminded that care for the most vulnerable is an act comparable to God's act in the exodus. Care for the orphan is an act that imitates God's care for Israel; the basis for this care is centered in the first commandment. Let us look more closely at the subtle relationship between mercy, piety, and care for the widow, orphan, and alien, beginning with the story that precedes the giving of the Ten Commandments in Deuteronomy.

In Genesis, the book that tells the story of so many vulnerable children,

God creates, blesses, and continues to sustain and renew creation. As an act of God's grace, God promises land and descendants to Abraham and Sarah. In Exodus, God reveals Godself to be one who is powerful and free to act in grace to deliver the distressed. The moral experience of the Israelites is shaped by this relationship with God: they are in a situation of distress in Egypt, are unexpectedly delivered from that distress, and their life in community is one of response to that event.[8] That response to the Exodus is shaped by mercy and piety: in joyful worship, borne from an attitude of gratitude and loyalty and expressed through community practices that are oriented toward God, and in taking care with their neighbor in a way that imitates the good that God has done for them. Both of these responses are grounded in a consciousness of humility as they remember their past.

God seems to know that there is a danger that the community will forget its distress, become comfortable in its freedom, and fail to extend to its most vulnerable members the care that God has already extended to the whole community. Including the widow, the orphan, and the resident alien in worship and festivals, and caring for their physical needs, tests the fullness of the community's response to God's act in the Exodus. The early laws that ground Israel's first covenant with God in the book of Exodus include a severe injunction against the Israelites' exploitation of resident aliens, widows, and orphans. The injunction portrays God as one who protects the vulnerable and destroys those who do not remember the plight from which God rescued Israel. In the widow, orphan, and resident alien God expects the Israelites to see themselves and to remember their ancestors' oppression in Egypt. The Israelites are to treat the widow, orphan, and resident alien with the care they wished their ancestors had received (Exodus 22:21-24).

Moses concludes this story by reemphasizing the significance of God's nature as protector of the vulnerable. The people are to imitate God through their actions of justice:

So now, O Israel, what does the Lord your God require of you? Only to fear the Lord your God, to walk in all his ways, to love him, to serve the Lord your God with all your heart and with all your soul, and to keep the commandments of the Lord your God. . . . Circumcise, then, the foreskin of your heart, and do not be stubborn any longer. For the Lord your God is God of gods and Lord of lords, the great God, mighty and awesome, who is not partial and takes no bribe, who executes justice for the orphan and the widow, and who loves the strangers, providing them food and clothing. You shall also love the stranger, for you were strangers in the land of Egypt. (Deuteronomy 10:12-13, 16-22)

Recognizing the just nature of God, and conforming human nature to God's nature, is the faithful responsibility of the Israelite people.

THE RIGHT RELATION OF THE WORK OF MERCY
AND THE WORK OF PIETY

Mercy and piety are directly related to the basic law. The interpretation of the law specifies the care for one another by which the people are to live. The interpretation includes cultic laws, or instructions for worshiping together, and social laws that order the activities of everyday life. Some laws protect the orphan, the widow, and the resident alien from unfair treatment in the economy that supports life. Employers must pay their poor and needy laborers what they have earned in a timely manner. A person of means should not take a widow's garment as collateral for what she owes. Israelites are to recall that phrase in the first commandment: "Remember that you were a slave in Egypt and the Lord your God redeemed you from there; therefore, I command you to do this" (Deuteronomy 24:14-22). Portions of crops should be left in the fields to be gleaned by those in need, placing the responsibility for making provisions available for the "widow, orphan, and resident alien" on the person with crops and fields. The poor cannot be accused of stealing from fields, for they are taking a remainder that is their due. Doing mercy is an act of personal piety.

These social responsibilities are related to true communal piety. Many of the religious practices in which orphans are mentioned show how ethical behavior and care for the orphan intersect with the communal worship of a God who protects the vulnerable. The widow, orphan, and resident alien are to be cared for through worship and included in all festivals and worship celebrations. In prescribed ways, the care of the vulnerable is at the heart of the practice of communal piety (Deuteronomy 14:28-29; 16:9, 11-15; 26:12-15; 27:19).

The books of the law introduce a vision of divine nature and human community in which God and God's community protect the vulnerable, include them in community celebrations, care for their needs, and treat them fairly even when they are easily cast aside or exploited. These moral practices cannot be separated from worship. It is in God's nature to defend the vulnerable, as God did in the exodus, and it is this nature of God that is worthy to be praised.

THE ORPHAN IN POETICAL LITERATURE:
THE CHARACTER OF HUMANITY AND THE CHARACTER OF GOD

Human beings do not live up to the vision of care and concern for God and humanity that is so central to the law, but according to the biblical poets, even God seems to falter. To the agony of the just, God in God's freedom does not continue directly to intervene for the protection of the poor and the just. Neither are human beings necessarily rewarded for living up to the law. Even so, the ethical mandate for community care of the orphan, and the hope that God will provide, permeates the vision of the faithful.

The book of Job provides testimony to the importance of the care of the widow and the orphan, especially within wisdom literature. In the last chapter we examined the innocent suffering of Job and the response of his friends as an example of narrative pastoral theology. In this chapter, as a pastoral theologian, I want to stress the assumption that Job and his friends share—that the righteous man cares for the widow and the orphan, does not exploit their vulnerability just because he has the power to do so, but comes to their aid. Job grieves for the days in which he acted in accord with what he believed the nature of God to be. In those days he deserved honor as a just man who protected the vulnerable, including the orphan (Job 31:16-23).

> "If I have withheld anything that the poor desired,
>   or have caused the eyes of the widow to fail,
> or have eaten my morsel alone,
>   and the orphan has not eaten from it—
> for from my youth I reared the orphan like a father,
>   and from my mother's womb I guided the widow—
> if I have seen anyone perish for lack of clothing,
>   or a poor person without covering,
> whose loins have not blessed me,
>   and who was not warmed with the fleece of my sheep;
> if I have raised my hand against the orphan,
>   because I saw I had supporters at the gate;
> then let my shoulder blade fall from my shoulder,
>   and let my arm be broken from its socket.
> For I was in terror of calamity from God,
>   and I could not have faced his majesty." (Job 31:16-23)

Who is the person of righteous character? A person of character acts in accord with mercy. A person of character is unwavering in care of the widow and orphan. Throughout these passages, the vision of the good life in which God and humanity care for, rather than oppress and exploit, the most vulnerable of persons, is unquestioned.[9]

The Psalms reflect the belief that God is defender of the orphan. In Psalm 94, the psalmist, who wants God to act with vengeance toward those who oppress orphans and others, agonizes. Similar grief is expressed in Psalm 10:

> Why, O Lord, do you stand far off?
> > Why do you hide yourself in times of trouble?
> In arrogance the wicked persecute the poor—
> > But you do see! Indeed you note trouble and grief. . . .
> O Lord, you will hear the desire of the meek;
> > you will strengthen their heart,
> to do justice for the orphan and the oppressed,
> > so that those from earth may strike terror no more.
> > > (Psalm 10:1-2a, 14a, 17-18)

Other psalms celebrate God's intervention on behalf of the destitute. In Psalm 82 God is doing what Job believes that God should do: the psalmist writes that God has convened the heavenly council and is adjudicating the claims of the destitute. In Psalm 146 the psalmist announces that God is punishing the unjust. In Psalm 68 the psalmist affirms that persons who have lived justly have been rewarded. A psalmist who, like Job, is afflicted with accusations against his character, recognizes that destitution for his family is part of the curse that his enemies wish upon him. But he is able to call on God for strength in Psalm 109.

The poetical writings that refer to widows and orphans struggle with the nature of God. They do not waver in the expectation that God will be just, strengthening and protecting the orphan and punishing those who exploit the vulnerable. They wrestle, however, with the mixed report from human experience that God is actually acting as humanity had been led to expect after the teachings that surrounded the exodus. Is God who God says God is? Is faith and hope on behalf of the widow, the orphan, and the resident alien reliable? In part, the biblical poets contribute to piety by bringing honest doubt, existential suffering, and excruciating agony into the presence of God. Ultimately, these poetical writings dig deeper beneath the more obvious experience of humanity and divinity to a "second naivete" that all of God's ways are not obvious to humanity. The writers express the deepest grief and agony when God appears to be less than all that God's faithful expect, but they affirm faith and hope in the mystery of God's goodness, justice, and care.

THE ORPHAN IN PROPHETIC LITERATURE: REAFFIRMATION OF GOD'S EXPECTATIONS OF HUMANITY

The books of the prophets agree that God defends the vulnerable. Despite differing social and historical circumstances, the messages of the prophets contain some common themes. Israel has not lived up to the covenant that would make its community whole. Whether the community is acting in accordance with justice and righteousness, living by doing good and turning from evil, is judged by the welfare of the most vulnerable.[10]

Amos speaks of "the poor" rather than "the widow and the orphan," but his criticism on behalf of the poor is so significant that it cannot be ignored: "Hear this, you that trample on the needy, and bring to ruin the poor of the land" (see Amos 8:4-8). Addressing the same social situation, Hosea calls the people away from their pride, from placing false confidence in worldly powers. Hosea's message, however, is slightly more optimistic than that of Amos. He reaffirms God's divine nature and the divine promise that even the lowliest orphans can best trust in God: "Return, O Israel, to the LORD your God" (see Hosea 14:1-3).

The orphan appears in the book of Isaiah in three passages that speak to the concern for the orphan in a wealthy and corrupt monarchy. In these passages Isaiah is concerned that the deep interconnection between justice and worship, works of mercy and works of piety, has been severed. Human piety that ignores the protection of the orphan, and other needy, is meaningless. Human goodness cannot rest on humanity's willingness to praise God and be separated from its holy living. Isaiah writes:

Hear the word of the LORD,
   you rulers of Sodom!
Listen to the teaching of our God,
   you people of Gomorrah!
What to me is the multitude of your sacrifices?
   says the LORD;
I have had enough of burnt offerings of rams
   and the fat of fed beasts;
I do not delight in the blood of bulls,
   or of lambs, or of goats.
When you stretch out your hands,
   I will hide my eyes from you;
even though you make many prayers,
   I will not listen;
   your hands are full of blood.

Wash yourselves; make yourselves clean;
   remove the evil of your doings
   from before my eyes;
cease to do evil,
   learn to do good;
seek justice,
   rescue the oppressed,
defend the orphan,
   plead for the widow.
Your princes are rebels
   and companions of thieves.
Everyone loves a bribe
   and runs after gifts.
They do not defend the orphan,
   and the widow's cause does not come before them.
(Isaiah 1:10-11, 15-17, 23)

Later, Isaiah offers a perspective not heard before. Anticipating the fall of Judah, he suggests that in a state of extreme godlessness, even the most vulnerable, the widows and orphans, are infected and will not be saved by God (Isaiah 9:16-17). Still, God will punish those who exploit the vulnerable; they will be called to account in the day of judgment (Isaiah 10:1-3). Isaiah, however, reintroduces the idea that the sign of God's presence comes through children, his own and a child of the house of David, Immanuel. He draws people to awareness of the presence of God by traveling about naked and barefoot, in the presence of his own children.[11]

The prophet Jeremiah speaks to the Judean situation during the decline of the monarchy and impending exile in Babylon. In some of his writings Jeremiah's agonies are like those of Job, wrestling with God's actions that seem to thwart the desires of the just, both in Jeremiah's personal fate as prophet and in the disaster awaiting the kingdom of Judea. As the people fall further from the ways of the covenant, and as Babylon becomes more of a political threat, Jeremiah's message of impending catastrophe strengthens (Jeremiah 5:28-29). But Jeremiah also envisions the possibility of repentance and renewal, especially, the reunion of mercy and piety. Jeremiah proclaims that care for the orphan, and other vulnerable persons, brings God into the presence of people, and people into the presence of God:

Thus says the LORD of hosts, the God of Israel: Amend your ways and your doings, and let me dwell with you in this place. Do not trust in these deceptive words: "This is the temple of the LORD, the temple of the LORD, the temple of the LORD."

For if you truly amend your ways and your doings, if you truly act justly one with another, if you do not oppress the alien, the orphan, and the widow, or shed innocent blood in this place, and if you do not go after other gods to your own hurt, then I will dwell with you in this place, in the land that I gave of old to your ancestors forever and ever. (Jeremiah 7:3-7)

The prophets, then, use the image of the orphan, among other images, to call people to a life that allows mercy to give birth to piety, to call people from making an idol of worldly power to faithfulness in God, and to renew a vision of fair treatment of the vulnerable and punishment for those who exploit that vulnerability. In contrast to a corrupt world, Zechariah presents an image of peace in which children play: "Thus says the Lord of hosts: Old men and old women shall again sit in the streets of Jerusalem, each with staff in hand because of their great age. And the streets of the city shall be full of boys and girls playing in its streets" (Zechariah 8:4-5).

THE NEW TESTAMENT: JESUS AS FULFILLMENT OF THE RIGHT RELATION BETWEEN MERCY, PIETY, AND CARE FOR THE AFFLICTED

Robert Coles's interviews with children reveal much about childhood theology and spirituality. Charlie, Junior, Junior's cousin, and Jennie, children who were interviewed by Coles in his book *The Spiritual Life of Children,* reflect on the existential dilemmas of loneliness, death, companionship, inspiration, and life. They conclude:

"[Jesus] taught everyone to love. He tried to love people; and some of them were glad, and they signed up to be with Him, and others, they didn't trust Him, and they were against Him from the start, and they never stopped being against Him. So He was all alone at the end of His life. They must have known He was special. It was His face, I guess, and what He said, and how He got to you. . . ."[12]

[after reflecting on Junior's sister's tragic death]: "What if God isn't really anyone! What if there's no heaven and no hell, either! No one can prove what he's like. . . ."

"If God isn't anyone, then maybe we're not either. At my [great] aunt's funeral the minister said 'ashes to ashes,' and I got scared. But if there's no God, that's all there is, ashes. No heaven and no hell. If God is someone, then we're someone too. He'll make us someone, if we let Him. I hope He will—that's what you pray for: that He'll be something for you, if you've given Him a chance, by being mostly good. You can't be all good, I know. . . ."

"You know, I guess the Lord and us, we're all in this together: us hoping to be saved, and Him wanting to save us"—delivered in an offhand manner as we ambled toward the door.[13]

These children are struggling with questions of law and grace, as did their predecessors—Matthew, Luke, and Paul. Their words bring a child's theology and spirituality to the eternal, existential questions that emerge in pastoral theology and should be answered by pastoral care—of life and death, of conflict and alienation, of oblivion and purpose, of comfort and wrath, of goodness and love, of mercy and piety. Junior, and all godchildren as they face sin and evil in the world, deserve from the Christian tradition a graceful answer. The question is: when the most vulnerable of children ask, will anyone be around to offer reassurance, in deed and in word? If there is, we will have retrieved the right relation of mercy and piety as the basis of our care.

Although I would not want to claim that the right relation of mercy, piety, and care of the afflicted is the only aspect of Jesus' life that is important to what it means to follow Jesus today, I do seek to demonstrate the following: this right relation is so central to the core of Jesus' ministry and the revelation of God in Jesus that if we lose sight of its importance, we distort the truth of who Jesus is and what it means to follow him. I will develop this idea, through the writings of Matthew and Luke in the Gospels and the Acts of the Apostles, and the writings of Paul in Romans—writings that seek to answer the question that Robert Coles's children raise.

MERCY, PIETY, AND CARE IN MATTHEW

The writer of the Gospel of Matthew announces early in Jesus' ministry that Jesus comes not "to abolish the law or the prophets . . . but to fulfill" (Matthew 5:17). Jesus as portrayed by Matthew fulfills the law and the prophets by maintaining in his ministry a right relation between mercy, piety, and care for the afflicted, the relation between humanity and God that is expected by the Hebrew Scriptures. This right relation reflects the close conformity of Jesus' human nature and God's nature, an attunement that arises from Jesus' intimate relationship with God. It brings Jesus into conflict with the religious authorities, resulting in his death. Jesus' example of the right relationship between mercy and piety becomes central to the lifestyle of those who follow in Jesus' way—it provides the reason for faith in Jesus, is basic to celebration of the sacraments, and is at the heart of discipleship.

Jesus' acts of mercy derive from Jesus' intimacy with God. In Matthew, Jesus' intimacy with God is well developed through works of piety, or devotional practice, before he establishes a ministry of healing the afflicted: he has been baptized by John, suffered temptations in the wilderness, and adopted John's ministry of repentance. Then, in Matthew 4:23-25, "proclaiming the good news of the kingdom" is linked to "curing every disease and every sickness," activities that result in his beginning fame. In the Sermon on the Mount (Matthew 5:1–7:27) and in the passages that follow, Jesus develops an ethic of care by and for the afflicted. To those afflicted with desires for vengeance, Jesus urges human love and generosity that never gives in to human retribution. To those afflicted with despair, he promises the kingdom through Beatitudes that unexpectedly console the afflicted's desperation with care and empathy. For those who care with the afflicted, he connects strength and resolve for witnessing to God with a quiet mercy and piety that seeks no ego gratification. These teachings reveal qualities such as peace, comfort, and humility, that allow the afflicted and those who care for them to maintain the right relation of mercy and piety. These teachings for the afflicted and those who care with them become the preparation for the challenges to come.

Jesus' ministry of mercy gradually brings him into conflict with the established piety of the Pharisees. Deeply attuned to God through his synagogue education, through the clarity with which he teaches the law and the prophets, and through practices of personal piety, Jesus engages in a ministry of mercy for the afflicted. This ministry of care is based on mutuality: he heals only the afflicted who seek him in faith, and he is changed when they seek him. The afflicted include the untouchables of society: the leper, the paralyzed, the feverish, and the demonically possessed. Through such care Jesus connects healing, faith, and the forgiveness of sins.

A mild challenge from the Pharisees begins, however, when he eats with "tax collectors and sinners." Jesus responds to the Pharisees by indicating for the first time that, when the choice must be made, his understanding of the Scriptures leads him to choose mercy over established piety, this time manifest as table fellowship with improper companions. He quotes the prophet Hosea in Matthew 9:13: "Go and learn what this means, 'I desire mercy, not sacrifice.'" He continues to respond to the crowds, always with compassion, concluding in 9:36: "When he saw the crowds, he had compassion for them, because they were harassed and helpless, like sheep without a shepherd." He disregards established religious customs, if necessary, as in Matthew 12. He repeats the reminder of the prophetic word from Hosea in Matthew 12:7 when he defends his disciples for plucking grain to eat on the Sabbath. He commissions the disciples for a ministry of mercy and healing, not for profit but for faith, in Matthew 10. He anticipates in a series of ways that such unconditional mercy and healing will produce conflict among kin, towns-people, and authorities, in Matthew 10:16-32.

Unconditional mercy and the conflict it creates with established piety is associated by Matthew with Jesus' unique personhood. In Matthew 11:3-4, John the Baptist asks, "Are you the one who is to come, or are we to wait for another?" Jesus answers John's inquiry with the evidence of works of mercy and the impending conflict with established piety: "Go and tell John what you hear and see: the blind receive their sight, the lame walk, the lepers are cleansed, the deaf hear, the dead are raised, and the poor have good news brought to them. And blessed is anyone who takes no offense at me." The evidence of consistent, unconditional mercy is all that is required to establish Jesus' identity for people of faith in God, such as John and the many afflicted. The reason for faith in Jesus is the example he is setting by the life he is living, in accord with the law and the prophets. Throughout Matthew 17, Jesus anticipates the death he will suffer for the life of mercy he is living.

Mercy and care yield genuine piety when a time of grief, compassion, and love produces acts that, for the Christian church, become sacramental practices. The feeding of the five thousand is commonly understood to have eucharistic significance, but it is also a genuine act of piety that *arises* from mercy, care, and compassion. After Jesus learns that John the Baptist is beheaded, he withdraws; the crowds follow nevertheless. He has compassion on them and heals them, but for the first time, he is also moved to feed them. The act of piety *arises* from Jesus' compassion and mercy. Matthew uses the phrase that becomes the blessing of the bread at the eucharist: "Taking the five loaves and the two fish, he looked up to heaven, and blessed and broke the loaves, and gave them to the disciples, and the disciples gave them to the crowds. And all ate and were filled" (Matthew 14:19-20*a;* see also Matthew 15:32-39).

Jesus makes it clear in Matthew 18 and 19 that a life of mercy is a life of giving away power. People accumulate and retain earthly power, for example, by holding on to status, their established group, their grudges, their sense of superiority over others, and their attachments to possessions. In a life of mercy people give away earthly power by giving up concerns for status in God's kingdom, by seeking the one who is lost, by forgiving others over and over again, by identifying with people of no earthly status, and by subordinating all earthly attachments to living a life that is attuned to God's will. Jesus has no compassion for those who seek power, such as the mother of the sons of Zebedee, who asks Jesus to bring her sons into positions of power in his kingdom; he has continuing, infinite compassion for the afflicted who seek his gift of mercy and healing in faith.

When Jesus enters Jerusalem for the last time he takes on the symbols of the kingdom of God: he enters Jerusalem on a donkey, he challenges the temple money changers, and he allows children to acclaim him as the Son of David. In the midst of these symbolic claims to his unique relationship to God, he continues his ministry of mercy. Although he often speaks in parables that most cannot understand, he becomes more explicit that the teachings of the temple are true but the established piety of the temple has been separated from a life of mercy and will not lead to God.

The contrast between established piety and genuine piety is summarized in Matthew 23:23: "Woe to you, scribes and Pharisees, hypocrites! For you tithe mint, dill, and cummin, and have neglected the weightier matters of the law: justice and mercy and faith. It is these you ought to have practiced without neglecting the others."

What can we conclude about the relationship of mercy, piety, and care from the Gospel of Matthew? The call to care is simple, but the consequences of care are complex. The simplicity: we are called by the Hebrew Scriptures and the life of Jesus to face-to-face, interpersonal care for the vulnerable, just what we have long understood pastoral care to be. The complexity: imitating the care of Jesus involves a life of unconditional mercy that includes sharing with those in need and making a place for all persons in communal celebrations, worship, and the most powerful of Christian symbols: the sacraments. When care is offered through works of mercy across the boundaries of established communities and in ways that transgress the power of established piety, simple acts of mercy may no longer be completely safe. Simple acts of mercy may require us to take on the vulnerability of others. Caring for the children of material poverty and the poverty of tenuous connections, strengthening their social ecology and supporting their rights, eventually requires courage.

MERCY, PIETY, AND CARE IN LUKE/ACTS

The two books written by Luke, the Gospel and the narrative of the Acts of the Apostles, develop the themes of mercy, piety, and care for the afflicted with a similar foundation but different emphases than Matthew. Luke continues the plumbline from the Hebrew Scriptures that shows the centrality in Jesus' ministry of mercy, genuine piety, and care for the afflicted, but he heightens the theme in some specific ways. Luke shows us a Jesus who does not wait for the Pharisees' reaction to his ministry but who actively confronts their established piety and the power it protects. Luke expands the rich theme found in Matthew of mercy as a foundation for sacramental practice, in his portrayal of both baptism and eucharist. In the beginning of Acts Luke shows that mercy and genuine piety are central to discipleship. As the book progresses, however, we get the first intimations that the conflict between mercy, established piety, and care for the afflicted will be a problem for the new Christians, just as it was for the Pharisees, Sadducees, scribes, and Jesus.

The birth narratives of Jesus and John the Baptist include a deft interweaving of the themes of the threat of separation, abandonment, or death to the child and his parents, and the promise, recited by Zechariah and Mary in the Benedictus and the Magnificat, that the lowly will be exalted.

Early in the Gospel the theme of doing mercy, and the conflict with established piety, is directly tied to repentance and sacramental practice through the preaching of John the Baptist. John preaches repentance: he warns the crowds that to repent means not depending on their established relationship to Abraham but practicing mercy as a way of life pleasing to God. He proclaims the coming of Jesus, baptizes the crowds, and baptizes Jesus. This action evokes, early in the Gospel of Luke, an association among repentance, practicing mercy, sacramental practice, and Jesus' unique personhood. When Jesus had been baptized and was praying, "a voice came from heaven, 'You are my Son, the Beloved; with you I am well pleased'" (Luke 3:22).

Jesus' teaching, early in the Gospel, announces that he fulfills the scriptures, both by his ministry of mercy that is consistent with the law, the psalms, and the prophets, and by his unique personhood (Luke 4:18-30). Immediately thereafter, Jesus' teaching and ministry of mercy are interwoven: as he teaches, he casts out demons, fevers, and other diseases (Luke 4:31-41; 5:12-15).

Jesus' conflict in his hometown foreshadows his conflict with the religious authorities that will begin immediately in the Gospel of Luke. A series of conflicts with the Pharisees and scribes develop in Luke 5:17–6:12. His mercy toward the afflicted sets aside established religious practice when mercy calls, and he shares table fellowship with all, including improper companions. The teaching that follows, the Sermon on the Plain (Luke 6:17-49), begins, as does the Sermon on the Mount, with teachings of mercy, but soon develops into provocative language. Jesus' wrath is turned on those who say they follow the law but do not practice it, and on those who say they follow Jesus, but do not follow his example.

Jesus engages in more work of mercy and John connects this work to Jesus' unique personhood, asking, "Are you the one who is to come, or are we to wait for another?" As in Matthew, Jesus responds indirectly, citing the evidence that the afflicted are healed: "And blessed is anyone who takes no offense at me" (Luke 7:23). Then, Luke condemns the Pharisees for their adherence to established piety that rejects mercy and portrays Jesus as the doer of perfect mercy (Luke 7:28-50).

The Gospel interweaves these themes and the expectations that, first, the disciples will have the faith to heal in Jesus' name (Luke 8:9-10); second, that the table fellowship of the sacraments is rooted in mercy (Luke 9:12-17); and, third, that Jesus is God's chosen son (Luke 9:18-49). In these passages, the disciples' lack of understanding also becomes evident: the disciples cannot effect healing in Jesus' name, do not understand the trials to come, cannot understand that following Jesus means renouncing status, and do not understand that anyone doing mercy in Jesus' name is on Jesus' side. Luke continues to weave Jesus' proclamation of peace, healing, and mercy, and builds both the sense of Jesus' greatness and the prospect of the crucifixion (Luke 9:51–11:36). When Jesus teaches, he is challenged by the Pharisees for his failure to observe customary ritual, and Jesus responds vehemently with woes to the Pharisees and scribes. In what follows, Jesus' language is increasingly condemnatory toward the Pharisees' lack of mercy.

As the Gospel projects an increasing sense of chaos, Jesus keeps a straight plumbline through the challenges to his ministry: doing mercy that leads to genuine piety, and the revelation of Jesus' unique personhood that is based on that relationship, should keep the disciples' priorities focused, even when the chaos leads to anxieties over the future and to division among kin. He cites a variety of ways that following his example and doing mercy creates division (Luke 12:1-59). He continues to interweave his teaching and direct acts of mercy that override established piety, in ways that threaten the Pharisees (Luke 13:10-35). In fact, as the metaphors heighten the tension, the absence of mercy predicts the wrath to come, as in the story of the rich man and Lazarus (Luke 16:19-25).

Mercy, as a sign of God, ought to be more convincing than the resurrection: Jesus suggests that those who cannot grasp the word through the law and prophets and through his example of mercy will not believe, even if someone returns from the dead (Luke 16:31).

The following chapters interweave, around the plumbline of unconditional works of mercy, the anticipation of the crucifixion and resurrection, warnings about established piety separate from mercy that destroys mercy, stories of genuine mercy, warnings about the transitoriness of riches, intimations of the sufferings to come, and the reliability of putting one's faith in God.

In chapter 22 the plots against Jesus by the chief priests and scribes occur in the context of preparations for the Passover, a practice of ritual and established piety that could be genuine but is shown to subvert mercy. The plot against Jesus is more important than the celebration of Passover. As they plot against Jesus, the chief priests and scribes are not fully aware of the crime against God and humanity in which they are participating, but the disciples are equally ignorant. Jesus celebrates the Last Supper, the most direct prototype of later eucharistic practice. Even after all of Jesus' teaching that mercy is at the center of a life in God and gives rise to genuine piety, and that eating together celebrates this mercy, Luke shows the disciples eating together in ignorance: after the Last Supper they still jockey for status and need to be reminded that the greatest must become like the youngest, the one with no status. Jesus' proclamation of mercy for all who have the faith to ask for it follows him all the way to the cross, as he forgives a criminal with whom he is put to death (Luke 23:42-43).

In the Gospel of Luke we find thorough development of the theme that mercy gives rise to genuine piety, and, when it conflicts with established piety, is the will of God. This plumbline runs through the Old Testament to Jesus' birth, teaching, ministry, and death on the cross. In the Acts of the Apostles, we find that this plumbline is carried successfully into the disciples' early, faithful ministry, and then is challenged as the demands of ministry arise. The message about care is again simple: acts of mercy that give rise to genuine piety are the will of God. But this message is more dramatic: the very needy are God's special children, and ignoring them is an affront to God Godself, an insult to God for which the comfortable will be condemned.

The Acts of the Apostles records the ministry in the name of Jesus by the disciples and others who gather around them. Initially, Luke's description of the apostles' ministry parallels his description of Jesus' ministry, and the themes of mercy and piety are fully interwoven. Peter's address at Pentecost proclaims that Pentecost is a fulfillment of the Scriptures, connects Jesus' "deeds of power, wonders, and signs that God did through him among you" (Acts 2:22) with Jesus' death and resurrection, and urges repentance and baptism of new believers. Those who believed "devoted themselves to the apostles' teaching and fellowship, to the breaking of bread and the prayers" (Acts 2:42). Unlike earlier, the believers now had the faith to heal in Jesus' name

(Acts 2:43-47). Their ministry was much like the ministry of Jesus, one of mercy and genuine piety, healing the afflicted, teaching repentance and faith in Jesus as the Messiah, and provoking the Pharisees and the Sadducees (Acts 3, 4). They evoke from the Pharisees the same response as Jesus did: the Pharisees consider them a threat to their power and try to silence them (Acts 4:17, 21, 29). The sense of wholeness of genuine piety and mercy among the believers is communicated:

> Now the whole group of those who believed were of one heart and soul, and no one claimed private ownership of any possessions, but everything they owned was held in common. With great power the apostles gave their testimony to the resurrection of the Lord Jesus, and great grace was upon them all. There was not a needy person among them, for as many as owned lands or houses sold them and brought the proceeds of what was sold. They laid it at the apostles' feet, and it was distributed to each as any had need. (Acts 4:32-35)

The story of Ananias and Sapphira suggests that this wholeness could not be maintained. On one hand, "many more wonders and signs are done among the people," and this ministry of the disciples, and the threat it creates to established piety and power, continues until the end of Acts. On the other hand, mercy is beginning to slip behind the demands of a new piety, even among the disciples, when in Acts 6 the Hellenists complain against the Hebrews that the widows are being neglected. Clearly, this is not the Christians' intention, and to correct the problem, Stephen and his followers are designated to care for the widows:

> And the twelve called together the whole community of the disciples and said, "It is not right that we should neglect the word of God in order to wait on tables. Therefore, friends, select from among yourselves seven men of good standing, full of the Spirit and of wisdom, whom we may appoint to this task, while we, for our part, will devote ourselves to prayer and to serving the word." (Acts 6:2-4)

But this action seems to be the first indication that even among the Christians, the relationship between mercy and piety begins to reverse, with a newly established piety—that of preaching and proclaiming Jesus—taking precedence over the ministry of mercy that, according to well-established pattern, becomes the one of lesser status. Does this mean that already the nascent church becomes confused about mercy and piety?

Yet Stephen's ministry of mercy integrates signs, wonders, and preaching Jesus of Nazareth, so that it threatens the Pharisees. When he defends himself before the high priest and the council, Stephen places Jesus of Nazareth in the story of Hebrew faith. As part of this story, he recalls Israel's status as "resident alien," a category of the vulnerable who are protected by the law and the prophets, and he refers back to Moses as the abandoned and adopted child of the Pharoah's daughter. These details of the story of Israel's redemption and the history of Israel's rejection of prophets who try to recall Israel to the law are connected by Stephen to Israel's rejection of Jesus of Nazareth. This speech is sufficient to incite the wrath of the authorities, and Stephen is stoned to death in the approving presence of the future apostle Paul. Stephen's last word is one of forgiveness: "Do not hold this sin against them" (Acts 7:60). Persecutions of the church begin, and the church disperses. Yet the ministry continues throughout Judea, Galilee, and Samaria, and mercy in the name of Jesus Christ continues in the stories of Aeneas, Dorcas, and Cornelius.

In Acts 10 the disciples are confronted with a new kind of mercy: that which preaches the Gospel beyond the bounds of the Jews. Peter receives a vision in which God declares, "What God has made clean, you must not call profane" (Acts 10:15). Again, the disciples will be called to a form of mercy that overrides established piety as the word will be preached to the Gentiles (Acts 10:33-43).

Challenges immediately arise to this message of inclusion, and these challenges dominate the remainder of the book of Acts and the writings of Paul. "When Peter went up to Jerusalem, the circumcised believers criticized him, saying, 'Why did you go to uncircumcised men and eat with them?'" (Acts 11:2-3). One hears in these words the overtones of the Pharisees' challenge to Jesus, "Why do you eat with tax collectors and sinners?" and all that phrase represents. Conflict arose each time Jesus' ministry of healing disregarded what Jesus considered artificial barriers to genuine faith and reconnection of men, women, and children with God. The book of Acts offers a warning and affirmation about care: even among convinced, practicing Christians, it is easy to subordinate and restrict care; yet the practice of inclusive care is a sacred trust, binding us with God and all humanity.

In the story and writings of Paul, Jesus (through visions) directs his followers to extend mercy across the bounds of established piety. He sends his message through the apostles to the circumcised adherents to the law and to uncircumcised converts alike. Ministry to the Gentiles becomes like an additional floor of a house that is still built on the foundation of the right relation of mercy and genuine piety.

PAUL

In terms of this book, grace creates the condition for the right relation of mercy and piety, one that allows the work of mercy and the work of piety to become the means of grace. Gifted by grace, and accepting that gift, one can fulfill the law and the prophets without the self-righteousness that becomes the basis of established piety that overruns mercy. To the Christians who are relying on strict adherence to the established pieties of the law and the prophets as the measure of salvation, Paul wants to point out that Jesus Christ offers salvation as a gift. Grace justifies. Paul is speaking of his own experience here: self-righteous adherence to the law and the prophets can actually create sin, as it did in his persecution of the Christians. Such a sin is so horrific that no human action can wipe it out. Yet sins are alike, large and small. Therefore, salvation is a free gift of grace, one that creates the condition for fulfilling the law and the prophets.

To the Christians who have no preestablished relation to the law and the prophets and may consider the law and the prophets as irrelevant to the Christian faith, Paul wants to emphasize that coming to faith in Christ connects one to the people who claim the faith that gives rise to the vision of life set forth in the covenant that God made with Abraham. This vision of life, as we have seen, has the right relation of mercy and piety at the heart of its teachings. It guides Jesus' example for his intimate relationship with God. When Christians accept the grace that is offered through Jesus Christ, they begin a process of transformation that guides them back to that vision for life. In other words, the right relation of mercy and piety in the law, the prophets of the Old Testament, and the teachings of Jesus lead one to grace, and accepting grace in one's life leads one back to the right relation of mercy and piety in the law and the prophets.

As Paul describes it, grace allows us to see ourselves as we are, in the fullness of sin and evil. Grace allows us to discover that our self-righteousness has blinded us, causing us to suppress the truth about ourselves and the world. What truth is that? "There is no one who is righteous, not even one" (Romans 3:10). To make this theology concrete to the topic at hand: all of us suppress the truth about our participation, individually and corporately, in the neglect and abandonment of poor children and the systems that make them poor. All of us are complicit in the abuse and misuse of children, through ignorance and neglect. In our everyday life we use concepts and participate in systems that, if they were evaluated for the way that they maintain children's poverty and neglect, would have to be radically reorganized. If we stopped, however, to do all the reconceptualizing and all the restructuring that is required for the flourishing of all children, we would be so engaged in years of "adult stuff" that we would neglect the direct, one-on-one attention that children require from within their biological and extended families and from adults beyond their families. Are we required to participate in systems of sin and evil, by the fact of living? Yes, we are. Within this environment, are individuals or small groups capable of extracating themselves from the systems that exploit? No, not very, because omission is as much a sin as commission. If we were judged by the results of our work, by the consequences of our daily actions for the flourishing of the world's children, would we stand condemned before God? We would. In fact, our situation is so hopeless that we may as well not try. We are inevitably the man who passed by Lazarus, leaving him to fend for himself.

But for grace. Grace is the gift that allows us to see our complicity and to use that knowledge for the sake of the good, rather than for our own self-condemnation. If God has removed our guilt and our shame, our works-righteousness and the despair that lies just beneath it, grace becomes the force that, little by little, produces the effort to change the way we live on behalf of the most vulnerable ones among us. Grace leads us to reevaluate our daily traffic patterns, our business as usual, to find the places where we can be present to all our godchildren. Grace also leads us to reevaluate the systems and ideas in which we participate, allowing us to see the consequences of our abstractions for the environment in which children live. Grace brings our basic desires into synchronicity with the divine desire for the flourishing of all.

CHAPTER FOUR

A Practical Theology
of Children and Poverty

Pastoral theology looks at the world honestly—with all its conflict, neglect, hatred, injustice—and holds out hope.[1] With hope as a constant in pastoral theology, pastoral care is well prepared to do the work of caring for children and poverty. Hope can be born in personal presence, conversation, economic opportunity, rebuilt institutions, restful activity, or liberating symbols. As development of the practice of ministry, pastoral care's strength has been in helping pastors and others learn to minister through personal presence, meaningful conversation, and liberating symbols; it has been less concerned with building community institutions, creating economic opportunity, or engaging activities in nature or the arts. If vulnerable children are at the ethical center of pastoral care, pastoral theology will need to expand its reach to make connections between the hope that is invited in presence and conversation and the hope that requires a wider range of activities.

In the day-to-day practice of the art of pastoral care in congregations and society, persons who seek to care with others are usually drawn into a continuum between presence, conversation, and action. In personal presence and meaningful conversation people may reveal that they need food and shelter, a job, time to be with friends and family, a way to be of service to neighbors, physical activity, a time to connect with nature, or a way to contribute their artistic gifts to the community. Caring may involve not only articulating the need but helping them connect with resources to fulfill that need. Strong established communities have well-publicized networking patterns that easily connect people with ways to express themselves and to contribute to others. In new, transitional, or declining communities, the patterns of living that connect people to hope-filled activity become less discernible. When communities decline economically or networking patterns fail, the community patterns that protect, supervise, and educate children, formally and informally, weaken. It is particularly easy for children to become the victims. Care through personal presence and meaningful conversation may be irrelevant unless we care with others by attending to care and hope through transforming institutions and communities.

Such an expanded understanding of care leads us to think about care from a practical theological perspective. Practical theology asks about ways to make connections among presence, meaning, and hope-filled activities. It builds a broad structure for thinking and acting theologically that allows us to make connections across a web of theological meanings and acts. It becomes a map on which to plot a direction. To care with people we may plan together a journey in a particular, hope-filling direction. That journey may point toward terrain that has not previously been mapped by persons whose primary job is reflection on care in ministry. The broad frameworks of practical theology help people who care with one another to share the responsibility for creating the journey. Some people know some parts of the terrain better than others; no one knows the whole. A caring journey requires cooperative knowledge. If practical theology helps provide a direction, it also helps us know whether we are prepared for the journey. An overall map helps us know when to travel with our present companions and when to find a guide with different knowledge.

Practical theology breaks the boundaries of what has been commonly understood to be the content of the discipline of pastoral care, yet it does so securely on the grounds of the accepted practice of good pastoral care. We have taught students of pastoral care that, in order to care with people interpersonally, the caregiver must follow the lead of the one for whom the caregiver cares, not taking responsibility for lives that others must live out, nor abdicating responsibility for our own participation in the emotions of a journey. In so teaching, we have prepared good caregivers to venture with relative safety into emotionally new territory. Such wisdom from pastoral care as it has been taught for many decades is infinitely transferable to strengthening and transforming the social ecology of communities. As we take shared responsibility for the journey we will use the practices in which pastoral care has built confidence, such as careful listening, attending to all present especially the less powerful, and building empathy. But we will practice care in new places where hope can be invited. This expanded understanding of care arises from the theology of earlier chapters of this book: if mercy is the center of care, and mercy is the origin of true piety or connection with God, then following the path of mercy wherever it leads is fundamental to caring with humanity and with God.

This chapter creates an expanded framework—a practical theological map—to help us find our way to the places that mercy and piety direct us. The means of grace are practiced, in personal presence, meaningful conversation, and hope-filled activity, in every location on this map. Each location may be a place of care in pastoral space—a space where God may be found and care with family, friends, neighbors, and strangers fills life with hope.[2]

A PRACTICAL THEOLOGY OF CHILDREN AND POVERTY BASED ON A SOCIAL ECOLOGY FOR PASTORAL CARE

Bronfenbrenner's social ecology theorized that the child (the microsystem) develops in relationships that are in direct relationship with the child (the mesosystem), the institutions in direct relationship with one another that have indirect impact on the child (the exosystem), and the culture in which the individual, the family, and institutions exist (the macrosystem). Whereas this general framework provides a good starting point, we can understand better the care of children and poverty by identifying systems that exist within or in relation to each of these larger systems.

In the child's mesosystem the family has been shown to have so much influence over children, potential and actualized, for good and for ill, that it must be thought about distinctly from other community institutions, including day care, that are directly related to the child. And for our purposes, congregations are particularly interesting as community institutions that have direct relationships with children. In addition, several layers of forces within the child's exosystem deserve special reflection. Local businesses that are the workplaces of parents, for example, or the private medical services available in an area, may be easily identified as part of a child's exosystem, but government offices, public policy making and enforcing bodies, including local, state, and federal, exercise a unique, sustained influence over families and community institutions. In addition to culture that may be regional or national, we now live in a global economy—a macrosystem that is informed by cultural beliefs but is increasingly maintained as an international structure of its own, ever less subject to governments. Finally, all care is dependent on the basic care of God through nature, the system that provides the home in which we live. Therefore, I imagine a relatively adequate social ecology for a practical theology of care to include seven levels: the individual child, the family, community institutions, government policy, cultural beliefs, values, and expressions, economic structures, and nature. In this chapter, I look at each of these seven systems, with attention to the following questions: How is pastoral care already informed by perspectives on each system and where does it need to augment its theoretical work? What practices do we need to engage and teach in order to help the religious community develop a general pastoral care that responds to the needs of children, especially those living in economic poverty and the poverty of tenuous connections?

THE CHILD AS INDIVIDUAL

Pastoral care in the twentieth century has made wide use of theories of the development of the child that have arisen in a series of psychological traditions, such as psychoanalytic, ego and developmental, narrative, object relations, and cognitive psychologies. Usually, these theories have helped us think about the care of adults. Some of these theories have been modified to account for gender, race, and ethnicity, but few differentiate issues of class.[3] On the basis of these theories pastoral care has created basic practices for caring relationships. For example, we have taught that human beings need caring relationships that provide consistency and presence, structure and limits, age-appropriate expectations, ritual and change, narratives that give us identity, and a sense of power to influence our environment. These theories have helped to create a practice of care through language, especially verbal counseling.

A large body of secular literature exists on the psychology and care of the child, especially addressing the social work profession. A few pastoral theologians have written about the ongoing development of children. For example, pastoral theologian Andrew Lester addresses the direct care of children in their usual development and calls for care beyond talk—care through play, visual and musical art, and other symbolically expressive forms. Some pastoral theologians address the counseling of children in special situations, such as bereavement. This topical work could be expanded to address the care of special populations of children, such as those protected by the Convention on the Rights of the Child. A popular literature is emerging that discusses the spiritual development of children. Very specialized research offers readings on the psychological effects of poverty on children, and this literature frequently does not take the church, religion, or spirituality into account.

Children who live with material poverty or the poverty of tenuous connections challenge our modern distinctions between childhood, adolescence, and adulthood. In the twentieth century, youth came to be understood as a time of advanced yet protected childhood, and young adulthood a time when persons who are prepared to establish families of their own leave home and gradually take on adult responsibilities. All too frequently, these developmental eras are collapsed. When experienced by youth and children, the problems that make adulthood difficult, such as inadequate health care and nutrition, family disruption, single parenthood, the need for continuing education and constant updating of marketable skills, responsibility for one's own and others' basic material needs, chemical dependency, domestic and community violence, and incarceration are particularly potent. We need to prepare ourselves to think about pastoral care with children who face this range of difficulties.

Internationally, children are killed by unsanitary water, malnutrition, health conditions related to birth and pregnancy, measles, and land mines.[4] Children's flourishing is thwarted by illiteracy and premature employment. According to UNICEF's *State of the World's Children, 1999* world peace and prosperity is threatened by illiteracy. "Providing education for all will cost only an additional $7 billion a year—less than is spent annually on cosmetics in the United States or ice cream in Europe."[5] Individual children die not only from lack of direct services for health and education but because national attitudes that devalue women and children prevent a child's flourishing from becoming a priority.

What can we do to share responsibility for and with children who live with material poverty and the poverty of tenuous connections? Our first job is to listen to the stories of childhood from the child's perspective—something adults do not do so well with any children. Reading autobiographical literature and ethnographies based on interviews with children provides a significant window into what we can expect if we listen carefully.[6] With these books as our guides, teachers, students in theological education, pastors, and laity in congregations can be emboldened to listen more directly to the existential, spiritual, and theological struggles of all children.

Then, we can reform the practices of the informal means of care for children that have been strained by our adult-centered and busy society. We can begin to see the children who are in our midst and to learn the kinds of practices that allow us to engage them as full members of our religious community. We can stop hiding behind the excuse that "we aren't good with children." Whereas some may be more called to the pastoral care of children than others, all of us can learn some basic practices that communicate respect for children, such as making it a habit to talk to a child at his or her eye level. We can cultivate a series of Christian virtues—patience, kindness, generosity, hospitality, compassion, joy—that create the spiritual space within us to receive children. We can habituate ourselves into not making promises we cannot keep and into being reliable with the promises and commitments we do make. We can cherish our work and hobbies and spend time with a child teaching and enjoying these avocations. We can allow ourselves to learn a child's avocations from him or her. We can think of the small ways to retain contact, even when our lives are busy, such as postcards and short telephone calls, in addition to face-to-face visits. We can pray for children. We can extend ourselves internationally through the many programs that provide the connections to support individual children abroad. Each of us can use our own imagination to think of ways to re-create the informal means of care for children who are already in our lives and to broaden our circle to children who are not.

In other words, the first step in the pastoral care of children is to think about broadening our own practice of the means of grace in our lives, beginning with "works of mercy." To crouch down to speak to a child at eye level, to stop our instinctive reactions to push a child aside and instead to think, How can I receive this child?, to teach a child to play a musical instrument or to take a child fishing is to open oneself to practice the means of grace in mercy and to open oneself to the presence of God in our relationship with a child. Once we experience the means of grace in this way, the possibilities for worshiping with children will emerge in a new light. We will no longer frame the debate about children in worship as one between the view that "children need to learn to sit quietly in worship" versus "children need their own experience that is meaningful to them." Rather, by re-creating our "works of mercy" with children, worship itself will express our relationship with children and will be transformed into a mutually shared and vital time of thanksgiving and joy.

Pastoral theology as an academic discipline, however, does need to think about the formal means of care that will allow us to prepare teachers and students to incorporate some bodies of specialized literature into its existing theoretical perspectives. In addition to teaching child development, we need to teach strategies that buffer children against risk—preventive strategies such as teaching children about basic nutrition, health, safety, sexuality, and the future. In continuing education and advanced programs pastoral care also needs to prepare ministers who can comfortably deal with the extreme difficulties of a child's life, such as loss and abandonment; physical, sexual, and psychological abuse; drug, alcohol, and media dependency; exposure to and perpetration of violence; and post-traumatic stress.

THE CHILD IN THE FAMILY

Pastoral care practice is well-informed by family systems theories and theories of the life cycle of the family. From these theories pastoral care has learned to think "systemically," or to pay attention not only to the individuals but also to the pathways of interactions among individuals and to the emotional fields created by the family system as a whole. Concepts from family systems theory such as the "identified patient" or "scapegoat," in which one individual, often a child, becomes the bearer of the conflicts of the family system, are common. The idea that generational patterns work their way into succeeding marital systems and have powerful effects on families has deeply influenced pastoral care practice. Pastoral care has relieved children from the burden of family dysfunction by caring for children indirectly, by strengthening and caring for adults through premarital counseling and in marital crisis, divorce, remarriage, and stepparenting. Pastoral care texts on families now attend to issues of different family structures, including gay and lesbian partnerships and families. Some pay attention to parenting, including single parenting by both sexes. Writers on pastoral care have recently produced texts specifically on mothering and fathering, and the care of women, men, and adolescents. In addition, using a broad practical theological perspective, the Family, Culture, and Religion project has produced twelve volumes that have examined family life from a range of biblical, theological, historical, and cultural perspectives.

It is a mistake to care for children without also caring for the adults who are their primary caretakers, but, in an adult centered society, we cannot assume that we can provide adequate care for children only by caring for adult caretakers. And, we must account for the importance of extended family and friends to the lives of children and adults. Teachers, doctors, ministers, activities leaders, and family friends, who come into direct contact with children also contribute to the resilience of children and their caretakers. Friends and family are important for "spelling" the parents and reducing their stress; for helping children through crises, including those that are exacerbated by developmental differentiation from parents; for helping children find their way into educational opportunities and jobs, and for role modeling and imagining a future. Much of the time, children who live in the poverty of tenuous connections have flourished because one or more adults took an interest in them. By learning how important extrafamilial adult relations are to the children who live in the most tenuous connections, we have been able to see that many materially well-off children live with inadequate involvement of adults beyond the biological family.

In many poor countries long periods of warfare destroy biological families and make extended and extrafamilial relations acutely important. But separation stretches even these relations to the breaking point. In more "stable" poor countries modernization and globalization place many stresses on nuclear and extended families. Former patterns of family formation, tradition, and values are deteriorating. Families become divided as they separate in search of livelihood, sometimes with mother and children remaining in agricultural areas while fathers seek work in the city, sometimes with mother and children remaining in one country while fathers seek educational opportunities in another. These separations are not only emotionally difficult, but infuse new and different values into a family. In Tanzania, religious women with whom I spoke were desperately concerned about the health risks involved in these separations. They recognized that men frequently became sexually active when their stays in cities were prolonged, and men brought sexually transmitted diseases home to their wives. In a patriarchal society, women could resist either the separations or the renewed sexual contact only with great courage.

How do we begin sharing responsibility for children with families in such a way that fragile families are strengthened? Once we have read about the lives of fragile families from their perspectives, we are better prepared to listen actively and to become supportive of persons in fragile families.[7] Then, sharing responsibility with mothers, fathers, and families means strengthening tenuous connections. Parents cannot really know the responsibility they have taken upon themselves until a child has arrived, with all of his or her particularities. In the most emotionally rich communities and congregations, parents can find others, within and outside the family, to help them with the challenges they face. Parents and children can be supported by other parents, families, singles, and retirees who are willing to listen and learn and to meet a parent at the point of his or her need. Sharing responsibility with families for the strengthening of family life means being ready to assist with parenting, providing formal and informal means through which to teach parenting, providing child care to reduce the stress of multiple expectations, and providing strength for parents through practices such as meditation and prayer. Sharing responsibility means assisting mothers to improve their mothering and fathers to improve their fathering, even when these persons are not married to one another. It means assisting those mothers and fathers, who are married to one another, through the hurdles and disappointments of married life.[8] Many programs are available to strengthen marriages that maximize the experiences of couples sharing with couples. Family-to-family sharing strengthens informal bonds of care.

On a more formal level, pastoral care will need to prepare ministers to understand and facilitate family intervention. Pastoral care education has long taught pastors about the patterns of alcohol and drug abuse, domestic violence, and child abuse. In addition, pastors should learn about the integrated family intervention efforts that help to stabilize fragile families. Family intervention supports families that are fragile as a result of multiple stressors. It aims at keeping families together who might otherwise disintegrate, either voluntarily through despair and stress or involuntarily through state intervention. It seeks to help families eliminate abuse and neglect by teaching parenting and family life skills and effective ways to respond to crisis.

My analysis of the family traditions described in Phyllis Airhart and Margaret Bendroth's historical study of families, *Faith Traditions and the Family,* showed that the major change in Protestant families in the United States in the twentieth century centered around family worship: persons in religious traditions that once practiced family worship and ritual had dropped the practice. Much work has been done on the misuse of the Bible and theology in families, especially as it is used to justify women's subordination and domestic violence.[9] These misuses of the Bible must be countered with positive models of "family spirituality," or positive practices of religiosity that constructively unify a family.

In a misguided attempt to strengthen the forms of family life, some popular movements today seek to stigmatize fragile families. Theologically, fragile families are of equal worth and have often become a means of God's grace, as we saw in Genesis and Luke. Biblical families, and the biblical heroes that emerge from them, are simultaneously wayward and faithful means through which God's grace becomes known to humankind. The work of valuing fragile families as God values them and strengthening fragile families for the flourishing God desires for them is a work of mercy that can become a conduit for God's grace, even today.

THE CHILD IN COMMUNITY INSTITUTIONS

A number of community institutions touch the child's life directly, and the strength of these institutions within a community provide a protective web around children and youth. Congregations, private and public schools, and other voluntary organizations (such as the Boy Scouts and Girl Scouts, Boys and Girls Clubs, organized sports and artistic activities, YMCA and YWCA, 4-H, and Rotary) provide religious and basic education, cultural experience, supervised activities, physical and artistic development, and connections to adults who help imagine and guide a child's future. The health of a community is almost directly measurable by the strength of this web. In economically thriving communities this organizational life is usually strong; in materially poor communities it is often thin or nonexistent. Often, the congregation is the last voluntary organization left in a poor community, and therefore, carries the weight of the community's hope.

In the United States the relationship between pastoral care and the congregation has been multidimensional at its best and distanced at its worst. The religion and health movement that was popular in congregations of the late nineteenth and early twentieth centuries spawned several models of pastoral care. One early model of pastoral care brought displaced children and youth into congregations and took religious workers into communities, a result of the ministries of the social gospel; such ministries eventually contributed to the development of the profession of social work.[10] Another model developed into institutional chaplaincy and served children and youth within institutions. Chaplaincy staffing in institutions was augmented by parish pastors, maintaining a slim congregational connection. A third model developed into outpatient clinical pastoral counseling that saw itself as an extension of parish pastoral counseling and was least likely to relate to children or low-income persons. The increasing deemphasis on the pastoral care of children and youth was also exacerbated by the increasing specialization of academic disciplines in the twentieth century, in which counseling was the work of (mostly male) pastors and care for children and youth became the work of (mostly female) Christian educators. Recently, interest in congregationally based care has reemerged among societies supporting professionalized pastoral care and counseling.[11] In addition, the congregation as a place to provide low-cost, preventive health care has been the focus of the parish nurse movement and the Health Ministries Association.[12]

The renewed interest in the congregation as a place of informal[13] and formal pastoral care may mark pastoral care's participation in a paradigm shift that has occurred among specialists in community organizations and in the care of families, youth, and children. Rather than thinking about communities in needs based terms, identifying weaknesses and pathologies that then must be corrected or cured, the new approach argues for thinking about strengths and assets that can be mobilized. During decades of research, John L. McKnight and John Kretzman of the Northwestern University Center for Policy Research have developed an asset-building approach to community development. At the center of this approach is the mapping and strengthening of informal associations in communities that are often overlooked by professionals who chart community networks.[14] McKnight and his associates use the asset-building approach, among other purposes, to support families and build child health.

Similarly, The Search Institute, an organization that does longitudinal research on adolescence, has developed a model of "asset building" for youth that provides a vision for the development of community resources that strengthen youth and families and compensate for risk factors in the environment. Search has identified forty personal and community assets and adapted them for congregational use.[15] In addition, Search provides training for congregations in asset building.

These approaches respond to criticism that the helping professions too often base their efforts only on needs or pathologies. Critics have long been concerned that the "helping professions" have developed symbiotic relationships with their "needy" clientele in order to justify their own efforts. Some have been concerned that professionalized helpers have disregarded or destroyed the persons in communities who are authoritative because they bear the community's wisdom. Others are concerned that professionalized helping creates a disempowering client relationship with needy persons. And, by labeling persons as "pathological" or "needy," the "helping" professions embed persons in an identity from which they have difficulty emerging to claim their strengths. Some persons criticize pastoral care and counseling for exactly these faults; others within pastoral care and counseling have been particularly concerned about issues related to empowerment and have sought to respond to such criticisms within existing perimeters of the pastoral work.

In a recent book, *Cultivating Wholeness: A Guide to Care and Counseling in Faith Communities,* Margaret Zipse Kornfeld offers an approach that helps bridge between congregational models of pastoral care and counseling and asset based community building.[16] Kornfeld presents a strengths-based approach to congregational care that deals with difficult issues head-on and recognizes the diversity in congregational life. In articulating this approach, she demonstrates that the counseling tradition has thought deeply about its contributions to the care that occurs within congregations, and she provides a thorough plumbing of the clinical tradition for the contribution it can make to congregational pastoral care. Kornfeld's approach builds a beginning bridge between congregational care and community organization.

This very brief description of the web of conversation and activity surrounding the idea of care through congregations and community institutions shows that significant activity, creativity, and fluidity exists in this area. At present, no one model dominates congregational care. Some approaches, such as that of the parish nurse movement, bring formal, preventive health care to the congregation in a way that has not been done before. In communities where professional services are thin or beyond the reach of low-income persons, congregational care could fill a large void in public health. Approaches such as asset building should bring renewed attention to the importance of the informal care of children and youth. Such care has traditionally been provided through congregational sponsorship of youth organizations, such as Boy Scouts, or through programs such as Vacation Bible School. When congregations either provide space for child and youth organizations to meet or directly sponsor such organizations, the visibility of such child and youth activities in congregations helps connect youth to those organizations. These organizations contribute directly to increased supervision, connection to adults, and future orientation of youth. Their importance cannot be underestimated.

In poor countries, the congregation is often at the center of community development. For example, in the Democratic Republic of the Congo, Bishop Ntambo Nkulu Ntanda seeks assistance in building congregational care with community networking features. With international financial support, a community church can be built. A $2000 contribution provides materials to build the church building, materials to build a parsonage, a Bible, bicycles for the pastor and the pastor's spouse, livestock, and a fishpond. This model builds on the community's strengths: financial assistance provides the materials and the local community provides the labor. With bicycles, a Bible, livestock, and fishpond the church can then become the center of a network of basic sustenance for the entire local community. This network will help to support and surround the local inhabitants whose families and communities have been devastated by war.

How can we share responsibility for children and youth through congregations and community organizations? In the section on families I reiterated that when we care for children or youth, we also need to care for the families from which children come and to which they will return. This principle needs to be extended to communities and the institutions and organizations that are important to the flourishing of children and youth. Persons who care for children and youth in congregations can initiate contact with persons in organizations that are providing child and youth programming on a regular basis. We can listen to their experiences and find out whether these organizations have a plan for helping children and youth who come with problems, especially when those problems are expressed behaviorally. We can ask whether all children, regardless of socioeconomic status, are welcome in such programs. We need to develop relationships of mutuality in and with those organizations, so that we can learn from them, create stronger communities with them, and be in a position to raise questions with them about what is and is not being done for children and youth, and why. If we engage in such conversations, desiring to learn from them, we will also discover the particularities of the social fabric that shapes the life of children and youth in our communities.

How might congregational participation in children's organized activities become a work of mercy? Congregations can participate in an evaluation of organized activities that insist that all children are valued participants and that activities should be conducted in the best interests of the child. We can join and support organizations with a "social screen"—a strong ethical base that extends welcome, generosity, and support for all children and communities.

For example, children and youth hunger for the opportunity to play organized, extracurricular sports, as the popularity of such sports shows. Some commentators have argued that organized youth activities overreach themselves into the overprogramming of young lives. Overprogramming negates the benefits of organized activity because it results in a lack of free playtime that diminishes child's creativity and imagination. Overorganized activities provide supervision but not the opportunity for emotional connection with adults.[17] But lack of organization and programming in some communities leaves children and youth energies undirected, unsupervised, and unconnected with adults. It is ironic that well-to-do communities may overprogram children, and poor communities may have too few directed activities, leaving youth unsupervised. This overly tight and overly loose web of organized activities for children and youth may be an interesting symptom of the increasing distance between the rich and the poor in the United States. Might congregational involvement bring some balance to such activities?

While thinking about youth programming that does exist through community organizations, congregations should think how their own programming intersects with the community. To use the previous example, sports leagues were once church based. The fact that children's leagues are largely independent of congregations, and frequently compete for the attention of children, youth, and their parents on Sunday mornings, may be a symptom of the increasingly tenuous connection between congregations and organized child and youth activities. While supporting the development of our own communities, we can also look for opportunities to support community development in countries where a small network of children's organized activities, which includes education, sports, art, and recreation, would be a dream come true.

CHILDREN, POVERTY, AND GOVERNMENT

Even though the United States formally separates church and state, dialogue with and even partnership between religious organizations and government for the purposes of care of children has a longer history than can be recounted here. In international child care, partnership between governmental organizations and nongovernmental organizations, including religious agencies, is a staple of care. Such partnering is especially significant for children's education and public health.

As the United States federal government grew in power, organized religious groups became involved in advocacy efforts with the government, creating a direct religious voice, providing information to congregations about national policies, and helping congregations become advocates for children. These important federal advocacy efforts continue. However, concurrent with pressure in the federal government to shift power to the states and to downsize government, a new relationship between government and the church has developed that potentially alters the practice of pastoral care.

The enduring legacy of Reaganomics has been a double-edged sword for pastoral care: government agencies have become increasingly open to working with religious congregations at the same time as they have become increasingly closed to employing religious personnel, such as chaplains, on government payrolls. When government payrolls were cut in Connecticut and Georgia in the early 1990s, chaplains were among the first to be discharged as salaried employees. In some cases the value of chaplains was known to local administrators, and chaplains were rehired as contract employees. The officials who had to put "smaller government" into practice also began to search for new ways of working with communities to fulfill their mandates.

The idea of creating health care through congregations was not new. For example, in the 1970s, under the leadership of a former United Methodist medical missionary to Bolivia, Dr. James Alley, the Georgia Department of Human Resources began to work with communities to solve health problems. One of Alley's goals was to decentralize health care as he had in Bolivia, bringing health care to people in local communities rather than requiring them to travel for care. His staff worked in partnership with trusted persons in rural communities who could make health care available in a way that persons far from health education could receive it. For Alley, however, health problems had spiritual dimensions. Alley raised the religious and ethical dimensions of public health problems with staff and in local communities.[18]

In 1980s, the Southern Governors Association began to engage congregations in efforts to solve community public health problems, such as high rates of infant mortality. Schools of public health and nursing also began to think about the possibilities of studying and teaching ways to work with local congregations to create better health conditions in communities. Sometimes congregations became vehicles to public health ends, rather than true partners in creating health care. Over time the concept of congregations as "partners" rather than "vehicles" became established.

In 1993, in a partnership project between the Georgia Department of Public Health and Candler School of Theology,[19] we introduced county health practitioners and seminary students to each other's work, gave the students six weeks of experience observing practitioners in their county departments, and then asked them to think together about the kinds of projects that might be cooperative projects in the local community. One congregational partnership developed support for single mothers and their infants; another sponsored an immunization clinic; a third gathered information for the development of a youth center. In the first case, a large, wealthy congregation discovered poverty within a mile of their church; in the second, a small congregation began a trend toward immunization in local congregations that significantly reduced the incidence of influenza in the county. In each of these cases, partnerships developed and, with minimal effort, important projects were begun. In the third, the student was unable to create a partnership. The student uncovered conflictive congregational and community dynamics, many of them related to struggles for turf of various community organizations that carried overtones of racism and prevented youth activities from occurring.

The movement among government officials toward communities was a precursor to a dramatic governmental decentralization, or devolution, in the late 1990s: the destruction of welfare entitlements in favor of a "welfare-to-work" program that was to be administered by the states. As state legislators scrambled to created programs before the federal deadlines, partnerships of community agencies worked together to draft proposals that would create a humane states' welfare-to-work system. These coalition groups often included religiously sponsored nonprofit agencies, and in that way, some of the voice and wisdom of the religious communities was heard.

For example, the recent religious involvement with creation of state welfare policies began in Tennessee with informal discussion among a Roman Catholic bishop, an Episcopal bishop, an executive with the Disciples of Christ, and a United Methodist bishop, Ken Carder. The religious leaders had several concerns about the welfare-to-work legislation that was being devised.

Inflammatory rhetoric was being used in reference to welfare recipients. Reforms seemed primarily motivated by saving government money. Provisions for job training, child care, and transportation for the newly employed were inadequate. Follow-up that would determine what had happened a year after people were removed from the welfare rolls was lacking. A safety net needed to be in place for the children of those adults who did not comply with the work provision.

Bishop Carder took these concerns to three United Methodist legislators, who were encouraged by interest from a mainline denomination. They agreed that an ecumenical approach would be best. Bishop Carder and his Roman Catholic, Episcopal, and Disciples of Christ colleagues requested an appointment with the governor to discuss their concerns. Prior to the meeting, they agreed on the principles of a just and compassionate welfare system in keeping with their Judeo-Christian heritage. At the center of those principles was priority given to the most vulnerable—children. The religious leaders shared those principles and asked whether the governor agreed. The governor publicly affirmed them.

That meeting led to three subsequent meetings between the religious leaders and the governor, his staff, and legislators; testimony before the House Committee on Children and Youth; and appointments to committees that oversaw the implementation of the new system, called Families First. The conversation expanded to include other religious leaders.

During the legislative process the religious leaders were in regular conversation with advocacy groups who were unable to get appointments with the governor. In a sense, the religious leaders became the spokespersons for the advocacy groups and the advocacy groups provided data for the religious leaders.

The religious leaders were also asked to participate in the state Advisory Council for Families First, a role that they agreed to rotate among themselves. Prior to the quarterly meetings of the Advisory Council, the religious leaders met with persons who were directly involved with the services of Families First. The leaders pooled the information they gleaned from the interviews and sought to bring realism to the Council about how well Families First was functioning. The leaders at times knew they were irritants to the Department of Human Services, but they also felt their viewpoint was respected. They also encouraged local religious leaders to express interest in the local councils that were being developed. Similar partnerships are developing elsewhere.

Many of the public health concerns in the United States that seem most intractable, such as infant mortality, violence and accidents, sexually transmitted diseases, chemical use and abuse, depression and mental illness, directly shape the lives of children and youth. Solving these problems requires government and community involvement, a partnership among many groups that work together at different aspects of the problem.

How do we prepare ourselves to share responsibility for children with government agencies? It is important to stress that we are called only to share responsibility with government, not to receive responsibility that some politicians would like to hand over to churches. Then, it is important to differentiate between politicians and government. Government is not a monolith of headline-making politicians. Government, like the church, is multilevel. In addition to politicians, it has officials who set the broad scope of policy, the perimeters within which care can take place. It has local practitioners who make room within that policy for responding to local needs, often stretching the perimeters a bit. It has educators who develop data, think critically, and create experimental projects. Most important, government is not them, but "us," members of congregations who are working on behalf of the rest of us. The stories of the work they do on behalf of children, youth, and families, in public health and welfare, protective services, juvenile justice, family courts, medical and legal services, can help to provide important, experience-near education to congregations about the role that government plays in the care of our communities.

Therefore, the congregation's role with government exists at many levels. Advocacy for the creation of sound policy can occur on local, state, and federal levels. While advocacy has been practiced successfully over decades, the Internet now makes it significantly easier to get current information about how an individual can become involved with church advocacy efforts. Newer forms of partnerships, those that are formed with the practice of direct care in mind, are also emerging, although openness to such projects varies with the personnel involved. For example, congregations have created partnerships with public schools, caseworkers, county health educators, and prison officials, in order to provide direct care to children, youth, and families.

As a step toward shared responsibility, how might the new body of knowledge that is emerging from partnership efforts build on the existing strengths of pastoral care? Pastoral care can teach that local knowledge about the state and community government agencies that serve children is important. It can extend its present teaching about making trustworthy referrals apply as well to making referrals to government agencies. New pastors need to visit their government officials, to know who handles what kinds of emergencies, to develop relationships of trust, and to assess their competence before crises occur.

Both government and pastoral care can use new and existing practices to emphasize prevention, especially the way that lifestyle choices influence self-care and care for others. As a new practice, pastoral care might address issues of good nutrition and proper exercise as part of its basic education. Nutrition and exercise provide a basis of self-care for pastors and for preventive care in congregations—the kind of care that buffers people against stress, disease, emotional distress, and mental illness. Another preventive strategy, building self-esteem among children and youth, can be built on existing pastoral care practice. Esteem building provides an antidote to many of the social dysfunctions that are health concerns: violence, abuse, teen pregnancy, and educational deficiency. According to John Gates, Director, Mental Health Program, the Carter Center:

> Some teenage pregnancy programs, when you examine them closely, fundamentally teach a set of skills that includes academic performance, vocational performance, and other positive actions. They also build a sense of future and of self-esteem. And what you find is the program is successful not because it emphasizes the evil of unsafe sex or sex out of wedlock. Success comes because the programs give these teens a different view of the future; it's a future over which they have some control, and it's a future they desire. . . .
>
> When we examine interventions, we find the same types of actions are successful, whether we're dealing with violence, teenage pregnancy, or whatnot. The commonality—what ties all of this together—is the interventions that develop one's positive skills, attitudes, abilities, etc.[20]

New partnerships in the United States mirror a similar change in international relations. Formerly, the United Nations (UN) worked almost exclusively with governments. Since the end of the Cold War, the UN has developed a more expansive strategy of creating partnerships between governments, business, and humanitarian organizations. In a speech entitled "Sharing Responsibilities: Public, Private, and Civil Society," UNICEF director Carol Bellamy, following the lead of UN Secretary General Kofi Anan, argued for partnerships between the government, business, and nongovernmental organizations, cooperating when and where they can—where businesses meet the ethical principles of UNICEF, where nongovernmental organizations are given appropriate credit for their work, and where government holds up its end of the responsibility for making sure that development reaches the poorest countries and people.[21] A partnership with civil society can and should include the churches that have long been involved in international humanitarian efforts, many of whom have publicly announced their support for the Convention on the Rights of the Child.[22] Such partnerships are being reported in countries' progress reports.

An agenda for the international pastoral care of children can be created from a list of issues around which such partnerships might collaborate. Bellamy suggests three international goals for child survival and flourishing. They are:

- First, that we must ensure that infants begin life in good health—and that young children are nurtured in a caring environment that enhances the physical, emotional, and intellectual capacities that they must have to learn and to grow.
- Second, that all children must be educated—which means that they must have access to basic quality education.
- Third, that we must ensure that adolescents have ample opportunities to develop and participate in a safe and enabling environment.[23]

These general goals reflect the twenty-four health goals for children's and maternal health, to be achieved by the year 2000, that were created at the 1990 World Summit for Children. Physical health goals are among the first necessary to ensure child survival since, in poor countries, preventable diseases continue to debilitate children. Seventy percent of the eleven million children who die annually will die of five diseases: pneumonia, diarrhea, measles, malaria, and malnutrition. The World Health Organization estimates that five million deaths each year are preventable. Increasingly important, however, are goals related to children exposed to war. These goals, outlined in "A Peace and Security Agenda for Children," include, among others, ending the rising use of children as soldiers; banning the use of land mines; protecting children from the effects of economic sanctions; including children's interests in peace treaties; prosecuting war crimes against children, especially recruitment, rape, slaughter, and targeting their schools and hospitals. Meeting these goals would free an international pastoral care to build children's assets in education and culture; failing these goals, an international pastoral care is necessary that supports special assistance for recovery from trauma, loss and death, violence, physical and sexual abuse, and coping with disability.

UNICEF is grounded on ethical principles supporting children's rights as outlined in the Convention on the Rights of the Child, and it is clear that its partners must support and adhere to those principles. Similarly, viable partnerships between various levels of government and the church are those in which the church claims its values and determines whether its work with government can be self-understood as ministry. Ministry occurs in partnerships between government and congregations because a congregation deems the practice to be good work, a work of mercy, work that congregants are motivated to engage because it arises from their faith. As an expression of faith stance a congregation may adopt a school, volunteer in its classrooms, and provide general support for its programs. These ministries must be distinguished from proselytization in which specific religious beliefs are promoted. In many cases, congregational projects that are explicitly religious are not appropriate for government partnerships. Congregations will be more at ease without the restrictions that government may impose. The crucial question is whether a given partnership allows both parties to enter into a project on an equal basis, so that the church can be the church, doing its work as a ministry of mercy rather than as only a vehicle and resource of government.

CHILDREN, POVERTY, AND CULTURE

Culture, according to Clifford Geertz, is made up of those "webs of significance that [people] themselves have spun," and the analysis of culture is, therefore, "not an experimental science in search of law but an interpretive one in search of meaning."[24] Culture creates an assumptive world that shapes the world in which children live. What place do children have in our cultural meaning making, in the United States and internationally?

Some persons believe that children are at the margins of cultural meaning making throughout the world, since what adults say and do often ignores children's needs, strengths, and concerns. In a pastoral theological work *Regarding Children: A New Respect for Children and Families* Herbert Anderson and Susan B. Johnson argue that the dominant culture in the United States is one of indifference and contempt toward children. Anderson and Johnson explain this attitude historically and psychologically. Historically, in philosophy and religion, children were seen as less than human until they had the capacity to reason or as innately sinful and depraved, needing their wills to be broken for their own redemption. Psychologically, modern adults tend to identify what they do not like about themselves with children and therefore resent children's vulnerability and neediness.[25]

Such indifference and contempt seems to be universal and related to devaluing women as children's mothers. According to UNICEF, when men treat women well, the care for children increases; when men disdain women, children become expendable. Therefore, the Convention on the Rights of the

Child specifically identifies the girl child as one whose rights require extraordinary protection, and UNICEF collects gender specific data on health care and education.[26] In addition, UNICEF sponsors the safe motherhood initiative that builds "mother-friendly" societies through four actions: applying the provisions of human rights instruments; encouraging governments to make sustained social investments; establishing women-friendly health services; and engaging husbands, parents, in-laws, families, and neighbors in efforts to make communities mother-friendly.[27] Maternal health enhances the chances of children's physical survival; maternal literacy and education supports children's flourishing.

Whereas dominant cultures may devalue children and women, subcultures (such as that exemplified by the UNICEF community) counter these beliefs and at times have been able to make institutional and behavioral changes that improve children's and women's status.

In the United States and Europe the culture of the late nineteenth and early twentieth centuries created significant subcultures in which children were central. Late-nineteenth-century women's activism swept the United States and Europe, creating a culture of "social mothering." Social mothering promoted the idea that the concern for children, women, families, and the next generation should govern the reform of politics, government, capitalism, and personal mores. The movement produced at least two lasting effects: it helped to create a family-centered welfare state that remains strong in Europe and new child-centered professions in the United States.[28] When we criticize the welfare state and the helping professions, it is important to remember that the movements that created these systems were produced in part by women who sought to solve the significant social problems of their era.

After the American Civil War (1861–1865) dominant culture seemed to agree that the nation had a stake in providing for those who risked their lives for the next generation: soldiers who risked their lives in battle and mothers who risked their lives in childbirth. Theda Skocpol, in *Protecting Mothers and Soldiers: The Political Origins of Social Policy in the United States,* demonstrates that protective welfare policy in the United States originated in post–Civil War culture.[29] In the early twentieth century, as society moved from memories of the Civil War and its aftermath to economic expansion, this cultural belief waned and the legislation that expressed it became less popular, even as the countries of Europe were enacting broader social legislation to secure the livelihoods of their working men, women, and children.

Shortly after the turn of the century in Sweden, Ellen Key, a professor of

Western civilization and the philosophical architect of European family policy, articulated the views of a portion of women's subculture that children, regardless of the family structure from which they come, are important to society.[30] The state had an interest in being sure that all children flourished and should therefore provide for the basic needs of children while also ensuring women's freedoms. Eventually, policies were enacted in Sweden to ensure the support of all children, regardless of family structure. These policies created an expansive welfare state that many people with concern for the welfare of women and children have long considered a model structure.

Although the culture of the child and family pervaded and transformed almost all regions of the United States, it did not succeed in creating permanent policies in the United States in which the concern for the child was paramount. For a brief period in the 1920s it seemed that the United States would follow the European example. In 1912 activists succeeded in creating the "Children's Bureau" as a federal agency to "investigate and report . . . upon all matters pertaining to the welfare of children and child life among all classes of our people."[31] In 1921 the Shepard Towner Act was passed, creating legislation to support educational efforts, local health conferences, prenatal centers, and home visiting, to be administered by the Children's Bureau. These successes were the "joint political achievements of women reformers and widespread associations of married women."[32] By 1926 the activities were well established, and renewal of the legislation in 1927 was expected to be easy. The renewal was defeated, however, by a coalition of groups, most important of which was the American Medical Association. The AMA succeeded in convincing Congress that the maternal and public health activities of the (largely female run) Children's Bureau were properly the domain of the (usually male) private doctor. Rather than expanding the influence of the mother into the sphere of the state, as generations of women had worked to do, the AMA successfully spread its privatizing influence into the domain of childbirth and the home.[33]

Meantime, new professions arose and organized. The duties of mothering and child rearing that the Woman Movement had assumed were natural to women became professionalized, as home economics and child psychology created experts who began to make women's family functions something that should be formally learned. Social work emerged as a profession from the settlement house movement. Much of this flurry of rhetoric and activity sought to make the welfare of children more central in American culture.

How did minority and poor children fare in this culture of the child? After the Civil War many religious groups sought to provide education for poor and minority children, particularly in the South, and many minority women became educators and administrators of schools. They were undermined by groups such as the Ku Klux Klan that particularly harassed educators as part of their efforts to undermine newly freed slaves.[34] Many orphanages were created that cared for the orphans of war, but cultural values that supported removing children from poor families were alive as well. The outplacement of Native American children, for example, did not end until legislation in 1978 put the responsibility for custody of tribal children under the jurisdiction of tribes. The fate of children was often tied to the cultural assessment of their mothers as "deserving" or "undeserving" poor women.

So, despite significant subcultural movements in support of children, Anderson and Johnson are right about our indifference and even contempt toward children. But philosophy, religion, and psychology are only part of the cultural story. The beliefs, values, and attitudes perpetuated by politics, economics, and civil society have also contributed. In addition, efforts to value mothers and children have often been tainted by racism, classism, and elitism.

As we look at the countries in which extreme child poverty exists today, we discover that sexism, racism, ethnocentrism, and classism contribute greatly to children's poverty across the world. Although the specter of a direct confrontation between superpowers has receded, we now see the rise in warfare among nationalistic groups that is fueled by racial and ethnic hatred. One way to destroy a culture is to desecrate its women and children, so the rape of women and the conscription of poor children into the military are effective means of war. However, subcultures that value women and children also exist. For example, religious leaders from very poor African countries, men and women, often report that their cultures value children. They consider children to be the future of their societies, and often their practices of caring for children beyond their own families support their claims. In light of the dominance in these countries of patriarchal beliefs and attitudes toward women and children, these religious attitudes and practices may be considered the signs of hope within a significant subculture.

Max Weber, in *The Sociology of Religion,* wrote of the power of those persons sanctioned as religious caregivers to create culture: "Pastoral care in all its forms is the priests' real instrument of power, particularly over the workaday world, and it influences the conduct of life most powerfully when religion has achieved an ethical character."[35] How might pastoral care share responsibility for creating culture and transmitting values regarding children? Many of pastoral theology's most substantial efforts are "culture-creating" and seek to help the church and its care and counseling practitioners counter sexism and racism and become aware of the needs of diverse populations. Building on these efforts, poor children need to become one of the populations to which pastoral theology gives significant, culture-creating attention. Then, to value children's participation in culture, we need to empower rather than trivialize them. Children think about peace, war, tenderness, violence, friendship, hatred, greed, and generosity as profoundly as adults, and often with more simplicity and less defensiveness. For example, Carol Bellamy reports that the Children's Movement for Peace in Colombia proved that the right to survival and the right to peace was Colombian children's most profound concern, and conversation among children reactivated political discussion about peace.[36] As adult advocates, we need to ask how small and large decisions affect children. Again, Bellamy points out that children suffer extremely as a result of war. Yet the demobilization agreements that have ended war have not explicitly addressed the ways that children's rehabilitation must be cared for after war and during peace.[37] If decision makers are not prepared to make connections between their work and the care of children, adult advocates who seek to create a child-friendly culture need to be able to demonstrate how children are related to all decisions that are made.

What bodies of knowledge does pastoral care need in order to carry out this mission? To fulfill its culture-creating function, pastoral care needs to regain a historical consciousness. History is the cultural memory of society, just as individual memory and family tradition help us understand what shaped individuals and families. Pastoral care texts offer complex and sophisticated understandings of the way that sexism and racism have functioned historically and currently. These understandings are necessary for our culture-creating endeavor. But our history of care is far less nuanced and focuses on the care given by the (male) clergy. Pastoral care needs to reconceive its tradition within a fuller history of how pastoral space is created—not only as the care offered by the clergy, but also the care offered by the laity and by ecclesial and parachurch organizations, where children and the poor are far more likely to be the center of concern.

Furthermore, pastoral care can build on its other culture-creating tools, such as epistemology and rhetoric. Epistemology helps us understand the basis for knowledge that people find authoritative, and rhetoric helps us discover how people construct arguments in languages that they understand. Persons who have practiced effective pastoral care and counseling are masters at understanding the private epistemological and rhetorical worlds of those who are different from themselves. Yet in public conversations we too often construct our knowledge and our arguments for those of our own assumptive world. We must speak with those like ourselves to build any base of knowledge, but we must also learn to conduct public conversations with persons who are very unlike ourselves. Only then will we be prepared, or will we be able to prepare our students, to speak on behalf of children. Only then will we be able to persuade fellow congregants and decision makers of the importance of taking children into account.

CHILDREN, POVERTY, AND ECONOMICS

Some children are poor because their families are poor; others are poor because their countries are poor. Adequate care of the most vulnerable children within the United States and around the world requires that we integrate a working knowledge of the economy with pastoral care. The philosophy behind the global economy has become a powerful force, teaching adults and children what to believe about acquisition, social connection, and care. In that sense, the economy can create or dismantle a culture of care. Three sets of practices—practices related to the formal economy, relief agencies, and the informal economy—offer three ways of thinking about the economy, poverty, and care.

Market economics creates culture. Like theology, neoclassical economic theory has its anthropology, or its understanding of human nature's desires, motivations, and actions. In its purest form, the philosophy underlying market economics assumes that individuals are responsible for their own choices, that their choices will be good because they maximize their self-interest, and that those who maximize their self-interest contribute to the common good. Greed and narcissism are not sins but are human drives to be channeled and directed. Relationships are subordinated to acquisition, and care is not the responsibility of the marketplace. Gambling and the economy become different versions of calculated probabilities.[38] At this level, market philosophy competes directly with Christian teaching for the souls of children. It becomes a religion that worships an economic god.[39]

Not all economists agree with the premises of neoclassical economists. For example, Bob Goudzwaard and Harry de Lange in *Beyond Poverty and Affluence: Toward an Economy of Care* propose that economic theory return to its tradition in which the object of economics is the care of "people and their needs," based on an ethic of responsibility that pursues the interests of others rather than self-interest.[40] The tragic flaw of modern economics is its attempt to create its own inviolability by eliminating all information from its calculations that does not produce financial return. Many of the caring functions of society cannot be calculated in financial terms. If the needs of care become part of economic calculations, as they should be, economics can be revised with human care as its aim. Economics as the means of care will be consistent with its end. Therefore, economic priorities should be ordered as follows: "(1) meeting the needs of the *poor*; (2) reorienting the priorities of the *rich*; (3) giving due weight to the needs of *future generations*."[41] Goudzwaard and de Lange have in mind the poor as understood in this book: the desperately poor children and families of developing countries and the relatively poor of industrialized countries, especially children.

The question that looms is whether the economy will provide a supportive foundation for the care of children, families, and communities, or whether it will constrict their care. Prior to 1990 the people sought answers to this question by debating the merits of market, planned, or mixed economies. Which was more supportive of children and families: market economies that forced the family to bend the family's care to support the needs of the market, leaving individuals to fend for themselves, or welfare state economies that provided services that substitute for family care and potentially depersonalize it?[42] In the post–Cold War momentum of the decline of the welfare state and the rise of the global economy, the debate is framed differently: how is the formal economy responsible for the poverty of children, and how might it be restructured with the care of children in mind? What is the relationship between for-profit, nonprofit, and informal economic institutions in promoting a culture of care?

Globalization of the economy is commonly associated with the wealthy institutions and persons of the for-profit, formal economy. In the international religious conversation of the last two decades, The World Bank and the International Monetary Fund (IMF) have been criticized for their part in creating the enormous debt of the developing countries, dooming their children to absolute poverty. The World Bank and the IMF were established in the aftermath of World War II with the laudable goal of creating and governing an international, but largely northern, economy. As decolonization of the southern hemisphere occurred, new countries joined the IMF, a condition for gaining national development loans from the World Bank. Two criticisms seem particularly germane to the poverty of southern countries that directly influence such issues as health care and education for children. First, international trade and lending occurs by standards set by the World Bank and the IMF. Extremely poor countries are kept poor because northern countries with key currencies (the Japanese yen, the British pound, the Euro, and the United States dollar) can print and circulate money as they need it, now that the dollar is not backed by a gold standard. Countries that must always convert their local currencies into key currencies on international terms are at a significant disadvantage.[43] Second, the World Bank and IMF have "structural adjustment programs" that set requirements for loans, governed by the economic philosophy described above. They have not taken local conditions into account. Religious leaders have seen these programs as inappropriately narrow and confining for poor countries.[44]

Transnational corporations are criticized for using child labor that would be illegal in the United States, for failing to reinvest in the communities and countries in which they exist, for extracting the natural resources with little benefit to the local people and for creating wealth for a few from the labor of many, working conditions in developing countries that would be illegal in the United States, jobs at low wages in developing countries that reap high profits in the United States, a favorable climate for sex industries that are particularly enticing and destructive for poor young girls, and urbanization and modernization that destroys traditional communities and has horrific consequences in public health, particularly in the spread of HIV/AIDS and other sexually transmitted diseases. These problems have a direct bearing on the lives of children, the conditions of the environments in which they live, the community and family life that provides for their basic welfare, and, particularly, their individual health.

In the last half century nonprofit and nongovernmental relief organizations have arisen, in part sponsored by religious groups. Relief organizations have received their share of criticism. The primary question is whether a symbiotic relationship exists between northern, western capitalism and nonprofit and nongovernmental aid projects: does capitalism create the suffering that in turn becomes the reason for being for nonprofit and nongovernmental organizations that then must perpetuate themselves and capitalism?

Michael Taylor, the director of Christian Aid in England, has written a thorough review of the history of the theological and philosophical discussion of charity, paternalism, partnership, and empowerment in theologically based, nongovernmental and ecumenical agencies.[45] Taylor concludes that the ecumenical ideals of the North, in what they hoped to achieve in a just and fair relationship with the South, have fallen far short of their goal. The economic system that entrenches poor countries in poverty must be radically restructured. In the meantime, while desperation and emergencies exist, Taylor concludes, it would heap injustice on injustice if agencies did not provide relief in international emergencies.[46]

These criticisms of international aid organizations are similar to those that have been leveled at the helping professions in the United States, yet educational institutions in developing countries desire pastoral care and counseling programs, especially as they modernize. So it is instructive to note some of the analogies between the international discussion about the formal economy and its relationship with relief agencies, and conversations in the United States about the economy, helping professions, and care.

Pastoral care in the United States has been restructured by economic change, for example, when hospitals have reorganized, especially when non-profit religious hospitals have been taken over by for-profit companies, or when pastoral counseling clinics have debated whether to make themselves eligible for third party insurance payments or whether to become service providers for health maintenance organizations. The debates that arise from practice sometimes assume that the survival of current pastoral care practice in market driven institutions is a good thing; other times these discussions have more critically identified the value differences between ministry and for-profit institutions. The more pastoral care and counseling is drawn into the formal economy, however, the narrower its clientele and the less likely it is to be able to fulfill its ethical mandate to provide care as an extension arm of the congregation to all persons, regardless of their ability to pay.[47]

As we have seen, the emergence of strengths based approaches offers a new convergence between pastoral care and community development in the United States. Similarly, pastoral care in the United States might learn from and inform international agencies that both provide direct relief and act as civil society advocates. What puts persons in pastoral care and counseling or aid agencies in a position to be public advocates? Speaking of the knowledge gained through ecumenical programs, Keith Clements has described a particular kind of depth knowledge that the church accumulates about situations because it works on the ground, listening directly to people. This knowledge is the basis for advocacy for others, especially with powerful governments.[48] Pastoral care and counseling has the kind of on-the-ground knowledge that is similar to that which Clements describes. My hope is that in the new era, pastoral care and counseling will be as acutely engaged in informing itself about the structural situations that create suffering as the ecumenical, relief, and humanitarian agencies have been—and that we will share responsibility for the rearrangements of the economy that are presently occurring, rearrangements that have ramifications for children abroad and in the United States.

Much can be debated about problems in the international economy that need to be corrected for the sake of the world's children, but two emerging events seem to predict that change in international economic relations is possible. First, an international consensus seems to be building that some kind of debt relief package needs to be provided for the poorest countries in the year 2000. Some are hopeful that debt relief will occur—the details are being worked out even as I write this. Others think that present debt relief proposals are not far-reaching and will make little impact. And some commentators think that shared responsibility is making an impact on transnational corporations. Some corporations no longer consider it in their best interests to condone behavior in their overseas institutions that violates United States law, especially when children are involved. Multinational corporations have located franchises in developing countries where human rights abuses draw the attention of activists. Activists, including religious activists, have put such companies in an international spotlight, causing them to consider the business implications of their actions. As a result, corporations have begun to agree to codes of conduct that require their international subsidiaries to subscribe to behavior that would be in accord with United States child labor law. In the views of some, this momentum toward human rights in corporations is especially important in light of United States government delays in strengthening human rights legislation that is particularly important to children: ratifying the Convention on the Rights of the Child, and banning the use of land mines and the recruitment of child soldiers under age eighteen.[49] Nongovernmental organizations and religiously motivated persons have become part of the monitoring and auditing processes to which corporations have become willing to submit, in order to substantiate that they are truly complying with announced codes of conduct.

How can we practice pastoral care in order to begin to assume our share of responsibility for the way that global economics shapes children's care? First, we can become knowledgeable about macroeconomic alternatives to the present way the formal economy does business and about the role of policy and relief organizations, especially those that are religiously based, in the care of children internationally.[50] In our everyday lives, however, average people can help to build and support a local and international informal economy that even now is emerging "beneath" the formal economy. Projects related to this informal economy described by Rob van Drimmelen include alternative trade organizations that import items from small producers in the developing world; eco-wood, or logs harvested by cooperative organizations with sound environmental policies; self-help initiatives and cooperatives for the unemployed; local exchange trading systems, where goods and services are exchanged without cash; worker-owned companies, microenterprise and microcredit initiatives, and responsible investment funds that either invest with social screens or invest with community development in mind.[51] Supporting such projects is a hope-filled, merciful communal activity.

In the United States, African American congregations, in particular, support local projects in economic development. For example, First African American Episcopal Church in Los Angeles now sponsors one hundred and twenty local corporations to support the entrepeneurship of its congregants. In Rochester, New York, the Greater Rochester Council of Churches organized the Progressive Community Credit Union, which has spawned a microenterprise lending institution. According to Sister Beth LeValley, an organizer, commercial banks in Rochester have contributed the greatest amount of financial assets to the institution, but the largest number of individual contributors are religious individuals.

With the assistance of the National Federation of Community Development Credit Unions, an organization that has sponsored thirteen youth projects, the Progressive Youth Committee has developed two pilot youth programs, one in St. Monika's, a Roman Catholic school, and one at Edison High School, a public school. At St. Monika's, students are encouraged to take economic responsibility seriously through "Savings Tuesdays," when Progressive operates a "pony express" unit at the school. At Edison High School, Progressive has helped create a high school based credit union to serve as a teaching tool for the business department and to help train students in the skills of banking. The Edison High School credit union is the first credit union in the country located in a high school and run by high school students.

Some theologians believe that any merger of business and the church, just as any partnership of government and the church, will result in the church's inability to challenge exploitation at its base. Those persons prefer to develop an international civil society outside society as we know it.[52] But the search for the solution to daily problems is particularly acute when children are involved, when one's decisions determine not only one's own suffering but the suffering of dependents at times of their greatest vulnerability. That may be one of the reasons that many African American churches in the United States seem to be preaching a gospel of economic and spiritual empowerment. Warnings that whatever we do involves us in a sinful system, by sins of omission, commission, and the unforeseen consequences of actions many generations later, can either create paralysis or open our eyes to ways that we can carve out some space to make room for hopeful projects for children. The dilemma and a way forward is summed up by Garth Kasimu Baker-Fletcher in "Summarizing New Ground" in *Black Religion after the Million Man March:*

African American entrepreneurial adventures—under the influence of the community and family principles of *Ujima* (collective work and responsibility) and *Ujamaa* (cooperative economics) . . . have a unique opportunity to advance both the *particular interests* of African American communities and the *general interest* of the United States economy. Black Power might now revise the maxim What is good for the market is good for the country (a dictum that has previously excluded the interests of almost everyone except a very tiny elite of fabulously wealthy individuals!), to **What is economically healthy for Black Americans is good for all Americans.**

At the same time, because the March called on Africans from throughout the Diaspora to become aware of one another's economic, social, and political plight, the deeper message of the March may be **What is good for relatively privileged American Africans must be shared throughout the world.** . . . African American capitalists must be encouraged to find new ways of *contributing* to others and thereby expand narrow definitions of "self-interest," which tend to collapse into lifeless "bottom-line" profit margins.[53]

Theological debates about the role of economics, profit corporations, non-profit agencies, and community empowerment follow parallel lines in the international community and in the United States. The importance of these debates in creating a hopeful future for the care of children cannot be underestimated: when children believe they have a future, they refrain from much of the socially dysfunctional behavior that leads to early death, children bearing children, disease, and spiritual malaise.

CHILDREN, POVERTY, AND NATURE

Nature is the child's original playground; it has often been the environment that has solidified the youth's religious conversion or relationship with God. As civilized people destroy nature, we destroy our children's inheritance. "Consider the consequences of your actions for the seventh generation," we are warned by the wisdom of many Native Americans.[54] The earth is the original place of providence, of the abundance that God has provided for us. God cares for us through the earth. We care for future children by caring for the earth.

Goudzwaard and de Lange's economic theory argues for "sustainable development," or economic development that the earth can support. "Sustainable development" is a critical term in international development, as the Northern Hemisphere consumes the bulk of the earth's natural resources, and the South needs to use natural resources for its development. Poorer countries of the

South fear that the North will impose environmental restrictions on the South that add one more burden to the South's poverty, without changing northern habits of consumption. For Goudzwaard and de Lange, a complex answer to this problem is found in the theoretical idea that an "economics of care" is "an economics of enough." An act of care for poor countries, for ourselves as individuals, for others, and for future generations, especially, is if those with more practice contentment with having enough.

Agenda 21, the report from the United Nations Conference on the Environment and Development (UNCED), commonly known as the Earth Summit, links care for the earth with care for children and youth.[55] In projects that attend to the environment and development, the concerns of youth and children must not be lost: indeed, care for youth and children are a significant part of the calculation about what constitutes sustainable development. The report sees youth and children and their organizations as important voices in the decision making regarding the environment and development. It recommends, as a part of sustainable development, that governments promote youth education, employment, and involvement in the United Nations, and that governments fight human rights abuses against youth. It recognizes that sustainable development promotes a healthy social ecology in which children can develop and recommends that governments reach child-related goals of the 1990s in areas of environment and development, especially in health, nutrition, literacy, and poverty alleviation. Governments should encourage primary environmental care activities that address the basic needs of communities and improve the environment in households and communities for children. It recommends mobilizing children in the activities outlined above. These activities can be guided by government enforcement of the guidelines set forth in the Convention on the Rights of the Child, a treaty that is consistent with sustainable development.

Pastoral care has not ignored the fact that, theoretically, caring for nature is consistent with caring for human beings. Care for nature has a significant place in the theoretical framework of Larry Graham's *Care of Persons, Care of Worlds,* a theory of pastoral care done from a process theology perspective, and in Emmanuel Lartey's *In Living Colour: An Intercultural Approach to Pastoral Care and Counselling,* a theory of care that incorporates an intercultural, international perspective with spirituality at its core.[56] The practice of care of the earth as a practice of pastoral care has been most fully described in Howard Clinebell's recent book *Ecotherapy: Healing Ourselves, Healing the Earth.*

Clinebell suggests that an ecological spirituality is created in the reciprocity between our receiving nurture from nature and nurturing nature in return. Understanding this spirituality to have both preventive and curative qualities, Clinebell suggests that the mind-body-spirit relationship is strengthened by three principles that guide the practices of education and counseling in which this spirituality is nurtured: "(1) by becoming more fully, intentionally, and regularly nurtured by nature; (2) by becoming more aware of the larger meaning of [our] place in nature and in the universe (ecological spirituality); and (3) by becoming more involved in nurturing nature by active earth-caring.[57]

Clinebell points to the alienation in western consciousness that has been created by humanity's attempt to establish its separateness from nature and the intrapsychic and interpersonal reconciliation that can occur through our reconnection. From this alienation, exploitation of the earth arises, endangering not only the earth but the resources of the earth that provide for the flourishing of the next generations. This exploitation has consequences both for the children of this generation and for later generations. Separating ourselves from nature, we simultaneously exploit the vulnerable: children, poor communities, and the earth by placing the toxic waste of our civilization in their midst.

In *Ministering with the Earth,* Mary Elizabeth Moore articulates "sacred hopes" that seek: "to inspire the church to minister with the earth in all of its coming and going, its doing and being. To minister with the earth is to serve God in such a way that we care for the earth, receive from the earth, and join with the earth in praise of our Maker and in healing our planet."[58]

The practices that lead to environmental destruction also reveal the worst about western culture: our racism and classism. Moore writes that those persons and groups whose voices are silenced are also those persons most endangered by toxic waste. She cites a study by the United Church of Christ Commission for Racial Justice that demonstrates that 40 percent of the country's landfill capacity was found to be located in communities of people of color: Emelle, Alabama (78.9 percent black); Scotlandville, Louisiana (93 percent black); and Kettleman City, California (78.4 percent Hispanic, or Latino). The same study revealed that 60 percent of African Americans and Hispanic Americans live in communities with uncontrolled sites for dumping toxic wastes; approximately 50 percent of Asian Americans, Pacific Islanders, and Native Americans live in similar communities. Many of these people live in communities with more than one site. In short, the study indicated that race was the dominant variable in the location of toxic dumpsites, and the pattern was consistent across the United States.[59]

Those who are vulnerable and without voice, such as children, minorities, and nature itself, are subject to such violence. Yet, Clinebell argues, "We cannot love our children fully unless we also learn how to love nature in ways that will leave them a healthy planet."[60]

Where do we in pastoral care need to listen in order to reconnect ourselves with the nurture of nature and our own responsibilities for the care of the earth? First, children can guide us to a fuller awareness of the earth. On a particularly rainy canoe trip in the Boundary Waters Canoe Area, my godchildren Elizabeth and Katie and I spent the day cheering a soggy mayfly as it attempted to molt from its casing, dry its wings, and fly. We had watched this procedure, usually a matter of minutes, many times before. The dampness of the wings slowed the progress of this particular mayfly so that minutes that became hours became most of the day. With the resilience of a child, the mayfly persevered through the dark, late morning. By midafternoon the mayfly completed its labor and flew. By then, the entire camp of seven persons had been drawn into the suspense, periodically checking on the mayfly. We were greatly relieved, as if our partnership in the birth of this one mayfly symbolized our partnership with all of the mysterious and unknown processes of nature and the earth that we take for granted. As we become aware of the quantity of these and other taken for granted processes of nature, the most intimate, finite of beings in our ecological web suggests the presence of the One who is transcendent and infinite.

Despite the importance of camping in the history of religious experience in the United States, theologians have rarely reflected in a systematic way on what it is about the experience of camping that has made it a staple of religious experience. Such reflection is grist for the theological mill of pastoral theology. Clinebell and Moore's books are important steps toward that reflection—what is it about nature that makes nature such a powerful experience of God's care for us? What do we owe it in return? As we become child-friendly, can we also become nature-friendly, for the sake of children? Nature waits as if it were one of our abandoned children, one that is eager to provide us with such joy, if we can only open ourselves to it. Nature awaits our neglected children, to nurture and heal the abandoned ones that they may flourish. Behind nature, a prevenient God of mercy reaches toward us and toward the children, eager to become visible, yearning to make them visible, longing to help us make the most of our important yet temporary place on earth, to spread our wings and fly toward human flourishing, in compassion and thanksgiving, like the mayfly.

Nature is most encompassing of the ecological system that provides the matrix for the rest of our social ecology: our economic system, our global and regional cultures, our governments, our local communities, our families, and our individual lives. Without establishing the interconnectedness between nature and each of these other systems, we miss the fullness of care that we are called to receive and give—the care that God has provided for all the children of the earth. The fullness of God's earth suggests that no children or their families are intended to be—or need be—materially poor or tenuously connected.

CONCLUSION

When persons who practice pastoral care take on their share of responsibility for the future for children and youth, they will be drawn into discussions, organizations, and bodies of knowledge that may be new for them. Whereas the territory is new, the methods are not. The founders of early-twentieth-century pastoral care did, in relation to science and its emerging professions and institutions, exactly that which is now called for in relation to new bodies of knowledge and institutions. The founders of pastoral care went into communities, the hospitals, and other institutions, where they had neither acceptance nor a place at the table, learned by experience what they needed to know, and brought their unique perspectives into the fluidity of the situation. Are we not now called to do the same?

NOTES

INTRODUCTION

1. "America Answers Call to Help Kids," *Chronicle of Philanthropy,* April 23, 1998. This can be found on the Internet at http://philanthropy.com/articles.dir/i13.dir/13summit.htm.

1. A MAP OF CHILDREN'S POVERTIES

1. The entire United Nations Convention on the Rights of the Child can be found on the Internet at http://www.freethechildren.org/uncrcdoc.htm. A summary may be found at http://www.unicef.org/crc/coven.htm.

2. Michael Harrington, *The New American Poverty* (New York: Penguin Books, 1984), 8.

3. *The State of America's Children: A Report from the Children's Defense Fund* (Boston: Beacon Press, 1998), 103.

4. A statistical profile posted by the NCCP can be found at http://cpmnet.columbia.edu/dept/nccp.

5. The statistical profile posted by UNICEF and used for the following comparisons can be found at http://www.unicef.org/statis/.

6. The statistical profile posted by the Annie E. Casey Foundation, with national and state comparisons, can be found at www.aecf.org/kidscount.kc1999/. The UNESCO secondary school enrollment figures used by UNICEF are higher as they calculate total enrollment of all ages in secondary school, rather than drop out rates of teenagers usually enrolled in secondary school.

7. Children's Defense Fund, 1998, xii. These data are taken from a Children's Defense Fund report by Arloc Sherman, *Poverty Matters: The Cost of Child Poverty in America* (Children's Defense Fund, 1997), 3. The report can be found at the Children's Defense Fund home page on the Internet at http://www.childrensdefense.org/fairstart_povmat.html.

8. For an analysis of undercounted children, see Bill O'Hare, *The Overlooked Undercount: Children Missed in the Decennial Census* at http://www.aecf.org.

9. Urie Bronfenbrenner, *The Ecology of Human Development* (Cambridge: Harvard University Press, 1979), 159.

10. See bibliography at http://www.prainc.com/nrc/bibliographies/fam_child.htm.

11. Phyllis Kilbourn, ed., *Street Children: A Guide to Effective Ministry* (Monrovia, Calif.: MARC, 1997), 11.

12. Ibid.

13. Ibid., 151. See also Maureen Junker-Kenny and Norbert Mette, eds., *Little Children Suffer: Concilium 2* (Maryknoll: Orbis, 1996).

14. Panel discussion at the United Methodist Council of Bishops, St. Simon's Island, October, 1996.

15. *A Report from the Children's Defense Fund,* 122.

16. Richard P. Barth, Mark Courtney, Jill Duer Berrick, Vicky Abert, *From Child Abuse to Permanency Planning* (Hawthorne, N.Y.: Aldine de Gruyter, 1994), 3-11.

17. *A Report from the Children's Defense Fund,* 68.

18. Lenore Weitzman, *The Divorce Revolution: The Unexpected Social and Economic Consequences for Women and Children in the United States* (New York: The Free Press, 1985); Ruth Sidel, *Women and Children Last: The Plight of Poor Women in Affluent America* (New York: Penguin Books, 1986.)

19. Pamela Couture, *Blessed Are the Poor? Women's Poverty, Family Policy, and Practical Theology* (Nashville: Abingdon Press, 1991).

20. *A Report from the Children's Defense Fund,* 79.

21. See bibliography at http://hd.wsu.edu/publications/fathering/fathers.html.

22. See NCCP newsletters at http://cpmcnet.columbia.edu/dept/nccp.

23. NCCP, "Early Childhood Poverty: A Statistical Update: March, 1998 Edition: Facts at a Glance." http://cpmcnet.columbia.edu/dept/nccp.

24. Alex Kotlowitz, *There Are No Children Here: The Story of Two Boys Growing Up in the Other America* (New York: Anchor Books, 1992); Jonathan Kozol *Amazing Grace: The Lives of Children and the Conscience of a Nation* (New York: Crown, 1995).

25. Kozol, *Amazing Grace,* 180.

26. Jeanne Brooks-Gunn, Greg J. Duncan, and J. Lawrence Aber, *Neighborhood Poverty, vol. 1* (New York: Russell Sage Foundation, 1997), 68-69.

27. Alan Wolfe, *Whose Keeper? Social Science and Moral Obligation* (Berkeley, Calif.: University of California Press, 1989); Browning, et.al., *From Culture Wars to Consensus: Religion and the American Family Debate* (Louisville: Westminster John Knox Press, 1997), 247ff; Gephardt in Brooks-Gunn *Neighborhood Poverty,* 1:7.

28. James Garbarino, et. al., *Children in Danger: Coping with the Consequences of Community Violence* (San Francisco: Jossey-Bass, 1992), 130.

29. Robert M. Franklin, *Another Day's Journey: Black Churches Confronting the American Crisis* (Minneapolis: Fortress Press, 1997).

30. See http://www.search-institute.org.

31. Peter J. Pecora, James K. Whittaker, Anthony N. Maluccio with Richard P. Barth and Robert D. Plotnick, *The Child Welfare Challenge: Policy, Practice, and Research* (Hawthorne, New York: Aldine de Gruyter, 1992), 30.

32. Sheila F. Kamerman in Edward F. Zigler, Sharon Lynn Kagan, and Nancy W. Hall, eds., *Children, Families, and Government: Preparing for the Twenty-first Century* (Cambridge: Cambridge University Press, 1996).

33. Meryl Frank and Edward F. Zigler in *Children, Families, and Government.*

34. Ibid., 121.

35. Ibid., 9.

36. Pecora, *The Child Welfare Challenge,* 13-30.

37. Brooks-Gunn, *Neighborhood Poverty,* 1:54.

38. Couture, *Blessed Are The Poor?*

39. Ruby Takanishi in Zigler, *Children, Families, and Government,* 256.

40. See Mike A. Males, *Framing Youth: Ten Myths About the Next Generation* (Monroe, Me.: Common Courage Press, 1999).

41. Herbert Anderson and Susan B. Johnson, *Regarding Children: A New Respect for Children* (Louisville: Westminster John Knox Press, 1994).

42. Don S. Browning, *Religious Thought and the Modern Psychologies* (Minneapolis: Fortress Press, 1988); Robert Heilbroner, *Behind the Veil of Economics* (New York: W.W. Norton, 1989).

43. Bronfenbrenner, *The Ecology of Human Development.*

44. Brooks-Gunn, *Neighborhood Poverty,* 1:49ff.

2. FINDING GOD, FINDING GODCHILDREN

1. John Boswell, *The Kindness of Strangers: The Abandonment of Children in Western Europe from Late Antiquity to the Renaissance* (New York: Pantheon Books, 1988), 174, 191, 196, 211.

2. Ibid., 433.

3. James Garbarino, et.al., *Children in Danger: Coping with the Consequences of Community Violence* (San Francisco: Jossey-Bass, 1992), 33.

4. John Wesley, Sermon 98, "On Visiting the Sick," in *The Works of John Wesley,* Vol. 3 (Nashville: Abingdon Press, 1986), 385.

5. Ibid., 386.

6. Ibid., 387-88.

7. Ibid., 389-90.

8. The concept of the visitor as the apprentice to the one visited is adapted from the idea that in pastoral counseling the best supervisor is the person being counseled. For the language of apprenticeship I am grateful to Maxine Walker and the "Companions and Apprentices" Conference of the Wesleyan Center for Twenty-first Century Studies of Point Loma Nazarene University, San Diego, California, February 4-6, 1999.

9. Wesley, Sermon 92, "On Zeal," *Works,* 3:314.

10. Herbert Anderson and Edward Foley suggest that this link between piety and mercy, or in contemporary categories, between worship and pastoral care, is broken when worship becomes the place of God's stories with little connection to the human. See Herbert Anderson and Edward Foley, *Mighty Stories, Dangerous Rituals: Weaving Together the Human and the Divine* (San Francisco: Jossey-Bass, 1998), 149. See also Elaine Ramshaw, *Ritual and Pastoral Care* (Philadelphia: Fortress Press, 1987), and Ralph Underwood *Pastoral Care and the Means of Grace* (Minneapolis: Augsburg Fortress, 1993). Conversely, pastoral care can become the place of human stories with little connection to the divine. Mercy and piety, or pastoral care and worship become integrally related when the stories of the human and the divine are linked and celebrated.

11. Pamela D. Couture, "Revelation in Pastoral Theology: A Wesleyan Perspective," *Journal of Pastoral Theology* 9 (1999): 21-34.

12. Albert Cook Outler, *The Wesleyan Theological Heritage: Essays of Albert C. Outler* (Grand Rapids: Zondervan, 1991), 22-37; Randy Maddox, *Responsible Grace: John Wesley's Practical Theology* (Nashville: Kingswood Books, 1994), 28-29; Theodore Runyon, *The New Creation: John Wesley's Theology Today* (Nashville: Abingdon Press, 1998), 149-52; John Cobb, *Grace and Responsibility: A Wesleyan Theology for Today* (Nashville: Abingdon Press, 1995), 35-43; Kenneth J. Collins, *The Scripture Way of Salvation: The Heart of John Wesley's Theology* (Nashville: Abingdon Press, 1997), 19-20; Elsa Tamez, *The Amnesty of Grace: Justification by Faith from a Latin American Perspective* (Nashville: Abingdon Press, 1993).

13. Maddox, *Responsible Grace,* 26-35; Wesley, Sermon 119, "Walking by Faith and Walking by Sight," *Works,* 4:49.

14. Andrew Sung Park, *The Wounded Heart of God: The Asian Concept of Han and the Christian Doctrine of Sin* (Nashville: Abingdon Press, 1993), 15.

15. Ibid., 36.

16. Ibid., 19.

17. Ibid., 81.

18. Tracy Thompson, *The Beast: A Reckoning with Depression* (New York: G. P. Putnam's Sons, 1995), 273-74.

19. Wesley, Sermon 1, "Salvation by Faith"; Sermon 5, "Justification by Faith"; Sermon 12, "The Witness of Our Own Spirit," in *Works,* Vol. 1; Sermon 44, "Original Sin"; Sermon 45, "The New Birth"; in *Works,* Vol. 2; Sermon 85, "On Working Out Our Own Salvation"; in *Works,* Vol. 3; Sermon 129, "Heavenly Treasure in Earthen Vessels" in *Works,* Vol. 4.

20. Larry Graham in *Care of Persons, Care of Worlds* (Nashville: Abingdon Press, 1992) calls this idea bipolar power.

21. Jon Sobrino, *The Principle of Mercy: Taking the Crucified People from the Cross* (Maryknoll: Orbis, 1994), 10. Sobrino, writing from El Salvador, rejects the language that I am using of "works of mercy," seeing "the works of mercy" as charitable acts that absolve the conscience and prevent people from living their lives fully by "the principle of mercy." I agree with Sobrino that the Bible calls us to a life lived by the "the principle of mercy," but also retain the idea of "works of mercy" because calling people to the "works of mercy" can help to move them on their way toward "the principle of mercy." I am concerned that the northern church ignores mercy because it believes that works of piety are more fundamental and negate the need for works of mercy.

22. See Theodore Jennings, *Good News to the Poor: John Wesley's Evangelical Economics* (Nashville: Abingdon Press, 1990) for a reading of how pervasive the principle of mercy is in Wesley's life, thought, and practice. See also Theodore Runyon, ed., *Sanctification and Liberation: Liberation Theologies in Light of the Wesleyan Tradition* (Nashville: Abingdon, 1981).

23. Sobrino, *The Principle of Mercy,* 10.

3. MERCY, PIETY, AND CARE IN THE CHRISTIAN BIBLE

1. I use the term "Old Testament" to indicate that I am using Hebrew scriptures as Christian texts for a Christian audience. I use "Hebrew Scriptures" in places where biblical writers refer to sacred writings prior to the canonization of the Christian Bible.

2. Although the writers of the Old Testament make children visible, commentators on the Old Testament may not. I compared eighteen Bible dictionary entries for orphan, children, widow, and alien (or comparable terms: foreigner, stranger, or sojourner). Seventeen offered entries for aliens (or foreigners, strangers, or sojourners), thirteen provided entries for widow, ten offered entries for children, and only five had entries for orphan. "Orphan" entry is extensive in Bruce Metzger and Michael D. Coogan, *The Oxford Companion to the Bible* (New York: Oxford University Press, 1993). In three cases, J. D. Douglas, ed., *New Bible Dictionary* (Downers Grove, Ill.: Intervarsity Press, 1996); Madeline S. Miller and J. Lane Miller *Harper's Bible Dictionary* (New York: Harper & Row, 1973); and Watson Mills, ed., *The Mercer Dictionary of the Bible* (Macon, Ga.: Mercer University Press, 1990), "the fatherless" were mentioned with widows. Entries on children always discussed their place in marriage, family, or parental status. In only two entries were children mentioned as vunerable in and of themselves: in one, orphans were referred to in the article on "child"; Xavier Leon Dufair, ed., *Dictionary of Biblical Theology* (New York: Seabury Press, 1973) and in a second, the "powerlessness" of children is mentioned; David Noel Freedman, ed., *Anchor Bible Dictionary* (New York: Doubleday, 1992).

3. See bibliography in J. David Pleins, "Poor, Poverty in the Hebrew Bible" *Anchor Bible Dictionary,* Vol. 5, and Thomas Hanks, "Poor, Poverty in the New Testament" *Anchor Bible Dictionary,* Vol. 5.

4. J. David Pleins, "Poor, Poverty in the Hebrew Bible," 402.

5. Thomas Hanks, "Poor, Poverty in the New Testament," 414.

6. It is interesting to trace the increasingly small commentary on "the orphan" despite extensive commentary on "the poor" and "poverty."

7. Joseph A. Grassi, *Children's Liberation: A Biblical Perspective* (Collegeville: The Liturgical Press, 1991). See also Grassi's entry for "child, children" in *Anchor Bible Dictionary,* 1:904-07.

8. Bruce C. Birch, *Let Justice Roll Down: the Old Testament, Ethics, and the Christian Life* (Louisville: Westminster John Knox Press, 1991), 131.

9. Ibid., 332.

10. Ibid., 260.

11. Bernard Anderson, *Understanding the Old Testament,* 2nd ed. (Englewood Cliffs: Prentice Hall, 1966), 272.

12. Robert Coles, *The Spiritual Life of Children* (Boston: Houghton Mifflin, 1990), 219-20.

13. Ibid., 223-24.

4. A PRACTICAL THEOLOGY OF CHILDREN AND POVERTY

1. Hope is a frequent theme in pastoral theology. See, among others, Don Capps, *Agents of Hope* (Minneapolis: Fortress Press, 1995); Andrew D. Lester, *Hope in Pastoral Care and Counseling* (Louisville: Westminster John Knox Press, 1995); James Dittes, *Driven by Hope: Men and Meaning* (Louisville: Westminster John Knox Press, 1996); Mary Louise Bringle, *Despair: Sickness or Sin? Hopelessness and Healing in the Christian Life* (Nashville: Abingdon Press, 1990).

2. An interesting discussion of the idea of pastoral space can be found in Stephen Pattison, *A Vision of Pastoral Theology: In Search of Words that Resurrect the Dead* (Falkirk, United Kingdom: Pastoral Monographs, 1994), 9-11.

3. Donna Aguilera, though not a pastoral counselor, provides an introduction to therapeutic psychologies, with attention to child poverty, abuse, and neglect. See Donna Aguilera, *Crisis Intervention: Theory and Methodology,* 8th ed. (St. Louis: Mosby, 1998), 1-23, 77-79. Doman Lum provides a similar introduction from a social ecological perspective, with reference to differences in ethnicity. See Doman Lum, *Social Work Practice and People of Color: A Process Stage Approach* (Monterey, Calif.: Brooks-Cole, 1992).

4. See the following UNICEF reports, available from UNICEF or downloadable from the UNICEF website, http://www.unicef.org, under "other recent publications": "Measles: The Urban Challenge," "Humanitarian Response to Children, 1999," "Groundwater: The Invisible and Endangered Resource," "UNICEF Papers at the International Child Labour Conference," "The Silent Shout," "Child Rights Guide to the 1996 Land Mines Proposal," "Children's Rights and Habitat," "Report on the Impact of Armed Conflict on Children," etc.

5. UNICEF's report *The State of the World's Children, 1999* can be downloaded from the UNICEF website, http://www.unicef.org.

6. Autobiographical and biographical literature, such as Richard Wright, *Black Boy* (New York: Viking Press, 1991), Agnes Smedley, *Daughter of Earth: A Novel* (New York: Feminist Press, 1987), and Leelan Jones, Lloyd Newman, David Isay, and John Brooks, *Our America: Life and Death on the South Side of Chicago* (New York: Scribner, 1997) tells of the daily confrontation with disability and death that some teenagers face. Ethnographical studies by Johnathan Kozol and Robert Coles cover every aspect of childhood; selected listings are in the bibliography.

7. Studies such as Constance Willard Williams, *Black Teenage Mothers: Pregnancy and Child Rearing from Their Perspective* (Lexington: Lexington Books, 1991) show that teenage pregnancy is often an affirmation of life in the midst of death. See also Nancy Aires, "Teenage Mothers: Seduced and Abandoned" in Rochelle Lefkowitz and Ann Whithorn, *For Crying Out Loud: Women and Poverty in the United States* (New York: Pilgrim Press, 1986), 125-37. See also the UNICEF report on "Safe Motherhood: Building Mother-friendly Societies" and the NCCP reports on fathering.

8. The marriage and family life education movement offers an array of preventive programs that seek to educate young persons about the responsibilities of marriage and family, prepare them for marriage and buffer them against divorce, help couples who are struggling gain resilience and satisfaction in marriage, and provide the possibility that even severe marital problems can be rectified. According to John Gottmann, who has done longitudinal research on marriage, couples who survive and thrive know their areas of disagreement and are able to make "midcourse corrections" that help them reestablish marital satisfaction. See John Mordecai Gottmann, *What Predicts Divorce? The Relationship Between Marital Processes and Marital Outcomes* (Mahwah, N.J.: Lawrence Erlbaum Assoc., 1994), and Gottmann and Nan Silver, *Why Marriages Succeed or Fail: And How You Can Make Yours Last* (New York: Fireside, 1995). Although I support marriage education, it has limitations: many of the programs are financially beyond the reach of struggling families, and it at times overstates its importance, as if marriage education could replace all family support. The programs are significant, however. The programs have been summarized in Richard Hunt, et.al.'s new book, *Marriage Enrichment: Preparation, Mentoring, and Outreach* (Philadelphia: Brunner-Mazel, 1998) and can be found on the Internet at http://www.smartmarriages.com.

9. A graphic account of the use of the Bible to justify domestic violence is told by Hannah Nyala in *Point Last Seen: A Woman Tracker's Story* (Boston: Beacon Press, 1997).

10. Charles Gerkin's *Introduction to Pastoral Care* (Nashville: Abingdon Press, 1997) traces several trajectories in the development of pastoral care in the United States that show how different models of pastoral care have emerged.

11. See, for example, Pamela D. Couture, "The Context of Congregations: Pastoral Care in an Individualistic Context," and K. Brynolf Lyon, "What Is the Relevance of Congregational Studies for Pastoral Theology?" in Carolyn Stahl Bohler and James N. Poling, eds., "Congregational Care," *Journal of Pastoral Theology,* 2 (Summer 1992); Joretta L. Marshall, "Pastoral Care with Congregations in Social Stress," in Pamela D. Couture and Rodney J. Hunter, *Pastoral Care and Social Conflict: Essays in Honor of Charles V. Gerkin* (Nashville: Abingdon Press, 1995); C. W. Brister, *Pastoral Care in the Church,* 3rd edition (San Francisco: Harper San Francisco, 1992); Gene Fowler, "Studying Pastoral Care in Congregations: A Hermeneutical Approach" in the *Journal of Pastoral Care,* 51 (Winter 1997): 377-94; and Alan Dowie, "Identity and Culture in Congregations," in *Contact,* 125 (1998): 10-16.

12. In support of this effort the Interfaith Health Program at the Carter Center of Emory University provides a database of health-related congregational ministries. The purpose of this database is not only to chart what congregations are doing but to provide ways of helping congregations that want to develop new ministries gain the benefit of ideas that have already been tried. See http://www.ihpnet.org.

13. A good discussion of the importance of informal congregational care, under the idea of "neighbor-care," can be found in Judith L.Orr, "Hard Work, Hard Lovin', Hard Times, Hardly Worth It: Care of Working Class Men" in Christie Cozad Neuger and James Newton Poling, *The Care of Men* (Nashville: Abingdon Press, 1997), 85-88; and in Judith L. Orr, "Theological Home and the Work of Neighbor Care," *Journal of Pastoral Theology* 6 (1996): 119-26.

14. For an asset based, community building approach, see John P. Kretzmann with John L. McKnight, *Building Communities from the Inside Out: A Path Toward Finding and Mobilizing a Community's Assets* (Evanston: Northwestern University Center for Urban Affairs and

Policy Research, 1993). See also http://www.nwu.edu/IPR/abcd.html. See also "Partners in Concern," a focused volume on pastoral care and partnerships in *Contact* 100 (1989).

15. See http://www.search-institute.org.

16. Margaret Zipse Kornfeld, *Cultivating Wholeness: A Guide to Care and Counseling in Faith Communities* (New York: Continuum, 1998), 71-74.

17. Richard Louv, *Childhood's Future* (New York: Anchor Books, 1992).

18. These conclusions are based on interviews done with James Alley's staff after his death, as part of the Candler Congregational Studies project, funded by the Lilly Endowment.

19. This project was conducted under the auspices of the Candler Congegational Studies project. Mark Sciegaj and Mary Ann Zimmer provided help to create and direct the project.

20. John Gates, "Resilient Communities: The Power of Prevention," in *Strong Partners: Realigning Religious Health Assets for Community Health* (Atlanta: The Carter Center, 1997), 36.

21. Carol Bellamy, "Sharing responsibilities: public, private, and civil society," speech given to the Harvard International Development Conference, Cambridge, Massachusetts, April 16, 1999. The entire address can be read at http://www.unicef.org "executive speeches."

22. A partial list of religious organizations that have supported the Convention on the Rights of the Child include Catholic Charities USA, Christian Children's Fund, Church Women United in New Jersey, Clergy and Laity Concerned (Cleveland Chapter), Daughter's of Charity of St. Vincent De Paul, Greek Orthodox Church of North and South America, Hebrew Immigrant Aid Society, Lutheran World Relief, Mennonite Central Committee, Unitarian Universalist Service Committee, United Methodist Church, General Board of Global Ministries, United Church Center, and World Vision. Listed at http://www.unicef.org/crc/updates/us-endor.htm.

23. Carol Bellamy, "UNICEF Executive Board, June 1999" address to the annual meeting of the UNICEF executive board, New York, June 7, 1999.

24. Clifford Geertz, *Interpretation of Cultures* (New York: Basic Books, 1973), 5.

25. Herbert Anderson and Susan B. W. Johnson, *Regarding Children: A New Respect for Childhood and Families* (Louisville: Westminster John Knox Press, 1994). Similarly, Bonnie Miller-McLemore argues that American culture disdains mothering in *Also a Mother: Work and Family as a Theological Dilemma* (Nashville: Abingdon Press, 1994).

26. See "Girl's Education: A Key to the Future," at http://www.unicef.org/girlsed/.

27. See "Safe Motherhood," at http://www.unicef.org/safe/.

28. Pamela Couture, "Beyond Private and Public Patriarchy," in Anne Carr and Mary Stewart van Leewen, eds., *Religion, Feminism, and the Family* (Louisville: Westminster John Knox Press, 1996), 249-74.

29. Theda Skocpol, *Protecting Mothers and Soldiers: The Political Origins of Social Policy in the United States* (Cambridge: Belknap Press, 1992).

30. Couture, "Beyond Private and Public Patriarchy," 260-64.

31. *First Annual Report of the Chief, Children's Bureau to the Secretary of Labor for the Year Ended June 30, 1924,* cited in Skocpol, *Protecting Mothers and Soldiers,* 481.

32. Skocpol, *Protecting Mothers and Soldiers,* 481.

33. Ibid., 512-13.

34. Gerda Lerner, *Black Women in White America: A Documentary History* (New York: Vintage Books, 1973), 83-143.

35. Max Weber, *The Sociology of Religion* (Boston: Beacon Press, 1963), 75-76.

36. Carol Bellamy, "Children as Catalysts for Peace," executive address to the Hague Appeal for Peace, May 12, 1999.

37. Carol Bellamy, "A Peace and Security Agenda for Children," executive address to the Security Council's Open Briefing on the Protection of Civilians, February 12, 1999.

38. For the relationship between gambling and economic principles, see Timothy O'Brien,

Bad Debt: The Inside Story of the Glamour, Glitz, and Danger of America's Gambling Industry (New York: Random House/Times Business, 1998), 258-96.

39. See Douglas Meeks, *God the Economist: The Doctrine of God and Political Economy* (Minneapolis: Fortress Press, 1989); Bob Goudzwaard and Harry de Lange, *Beyond Poverty and Affluence: Toward an Economy of Care with a Twelve Step Program for Economic Recovery,* translated into English and edited by Mark R. Van der Vennen (Grand Rapids: Eerdmans, 1995); and Rob Van Drimmelen, *Faith in a Global Economy: A Primer for Christians* (Geneva: WCC Publications, 1998); Herman E. Daly and John B. Cobb, *For the Common Good: Redirecting the Economy Toward Community, the Environment, and a Sustainable Future* (Boston: Beacon Press, 1989); Barbara Rumscheidt, *No Room for Grace: Pastoral Theology and Dehumanization in the Global Economy* (Grand Rapids: Eerdmans, 1998).

40. Goudzwaard and de Lange, *Beyond Poverty and Affluence,* 69.

41. Ibid., 70.

42. For the discussion of the market family and the state family see Alan Wolfe, *Whose Keeper? Social Science and Moral Obligation* (Berkeley, Calif.: University of California Press, 1989), and Don S. Browning, Bonnie Miller-McLemore, Pamela Couture, K. Brynolf Lyon, and Robert M. Franklin, *From Culture Wars to Consensus: Religion and the American Family Debate* (Louisville: Westminster John Knox Press, 1997), 247-68.

43. For an accessible discussion of this complicated issue, see Goudzwaard and de Lange, *Beyond Poverty and Affluence,* 85-88.

44. For a balanced discussion of the history of these institutions and their policies as the Southern Hemisphere emerged, of the ways in which northern countries have created and even benefited from the southern debt crisis, with appropriate criticisms of problems in development in the southern countries, see van Drimmelen, *Faith in a Global Economy,* 51-74.

45. Michael Taylor, *Not Angels but Agencies: The Ecumenical Reponse to Poverty, A Primer* (Geneva: WCC Publications, 1995). His work is based on an evaluation by four agencies (Bread for the World, EZE in Germany, ICCO in the Netherlands, and Christian Aid) who also asked the World Council of Churches Communion on the Churches' Participation in Development to gather a group of experienced persons from the South to present their own perspective.

46. Ibid., 142-44.

47. See Pamela Couture and Richard Hester, "The Future of Pastoral Care and Counseling and the God of the Market," in Pamela D. Couture and Rodney Hunter, eds., *Pastoral Care and Social Conflict* (Nashville: Abingdon Press, 1995), 44-54.

48. Keith Clements, *Learning to Speak: The Church's Voice in Public Affairs* (Edinburgh: T & T Clark, 1995), 146.

49. Kenneth Roth, "Sidelined on Human Rights," in *Foreign Affairs* 77:2 (March/April 1998): 2-7; and Debora L. Spar, "The Spotlight and the Bottom Line," in *Foreign Affairs* 77:2 (March/April 1998): 7-13.

50. For example, see Goudzwaard and de Lange's twelve proposals for structural adjustments toward creating both a philosophy of and the structures for a caring economy, *Beyond Poverty and Affluence,* 134-61.

51. See van Drimmelen, *Faith in a Global Economy,* 138-55; Goudzwaard and de Lange, *Beyond Poverty and Affluence,* 134-61.

52. Taylor describes the debate: "Empowering people to exploit systems as much as to change them is controversial. Many of the Southern contributors to 'Discerning the Way Together' can be read as being strongly against it. For them this is the time 'to be excluded from the present order' and to build an 'international civil society' outside organized society as we know it. Their anti-systemic approach is not against all systems as such but is firmly opposed to this one 'which produces and excludes the poor at the same time.' They are also suspicious of a possible shift by Northern agencies away from a clear commitment to transformation toward

a more pragmatic attack on poverty. There is a fine line between playing by Western rules—adopting Western tactics and Western efficiency—in order to 'beat the system' and being finally co-opted by it." Taylor, *Not Angels but Agencies,* 146.

53. Garth Kasimu Baker-Fletcher, ed., *Black Religion after the Million Man March: Voices of the Future* (New York: Orbis, 1998), 162.

54. Native American theology offers perspectives on nature and creation that should help to build its place in pastoral counseling. For example, see George Tinker, "Spirituality, Native American Personhood, Sovereignty, and Solidarity," in James Treat, ed., *Native and Christian: Indigenous Voices in the United States and Canada* (New York: Routledge, 1996); and Jace Weaver, ed., *Defending Mother Earth: Native American Perspectives on Environmental Justice* (Maryknoll: Orbis, 1996).

55. Agenda 21, Report of the United Nations Conference on Environment and Development, Rio de Janiero, June 3-14, 1992. Available at gopher://nywork1.undp.org/11/unconfs/UNCED/English.

56. Larry Graham, *Care of Persons, Care of Worlds* (Nashville: Abingdon Press, 1992) and Emmanuel Y. Lartey, *In Living Colour: An Intercultural Approach to Pastoral Care and Counselling* (London: Cassell, 1997).

57. Howard Clinebell, *Ecotherapy: Healing Ourselves, Healing the Earth* (New York: The Haworth Press, 1996), 63.

58. Mary Elizabeth Moore, *Ministering with the Earth* (St. Louis: Chalice Press, 1998), 3.

59. Ibid., 121.

60. Clinebell, *Ecotherapy,* 79.

BOOKS

Aguilera, Donna C. *Crisis Intervention: Theory and Methodology.* 8th ed. St. Louis: Mosby, 1998.

Anderson, Bernard. *Understanding the Old Testament.* 2nd ed. Englewood Cliffs: Prentice Hall, 1966.

Anderson, Herbert and Susan B. Johnson. *Regarding Children: A New Respect for Children.* Louisville: Westminster John Knox Press, 1994.

Anderson, Herbert and Edward Foley. *Mighty Stories, Dangerous Rituals: Weaving Together the Human and the Divine.* San Francisco: Jossey-Bass, 1998.

Baker-Fletcher, Garth Kasimu, ed. *Black Religion after the Million Man March.* Maryknoll: Orbis, 1998.

Barth, Richard P., Mark Courtney, Jill Duerr Berrick, Vicky Abert. *From Child Abuse to Permanency Planning.* Hawthorne, New York: Aldine de Gruyter, 1994.

Birch, Bruce C. *Let Justice Roll Down: the Old Testament, Ethics, and the Christian Life.* Louisville: Westminster John Knox Press, 1991.

Blumenthal, David. *Facing the Abusing God: A Theory of Protest.* Louisville: Westminster John Knox Press, 1993.

Boswell, John. *The Kindness of Strangers: The Abandonment of Children in Western Europe from Late Antiquity to the Renaissance.* New York: Pantheon Books, 1988.

Bringle, Mary Louise. *Despair: Sickness or Sin? Hopelessness and Healing.* Nashville: Abingdon Press, 1990.

Brister, C. W. *Pastoral Care in the Church.* 3rd ed. San Francisco: HarperSanFrancisco, 1992.

Bronfenbrenner, Urie. *The Ecology of Human Development.* Cambridge: Harvard University Press, 1979.

Brooks-Gunn, Jeanne, Greg J. Duncan, J. Lawrence Aber, eds. *Neighborhood Poverty.* 2 volumes. New York: Russell Sage Foundation, 1997.

Brown, Joanne Carlson, and Carole Bohn, ed. *Christianity, Patriarchy, and Abuse.* New York: Pilgrim Press, 1989.

Browning, Don S., Bonnie J. Miller-McLemore, Pamela D. Couture, K. Brynolf Lyon, and Robert M. Franklin. *From Culture Wars to Common Ground: Religions and the American Family Debate.* Louisville: Westminster John Knox Press, 1997.

Browning, Don S. *Religious Thought and the Modern Psychologies.* Minneapolis: Fortress Press, 1988.

Byrd, Walter and Paul Warren, M.D. *Counseling and Children: Resources for Christian Counseling.* Dallas: Word, 1989.

Capps, Don. *Agents of Hope: A Pastoral Theology.* Minneapolis: Fortress Press, 1995.

Capps, Donald. *The Child's Song: The Religious Abuse of Children.* Louisville: Westminster John Knox, 1995.

Clements, Keith. *Learning to Speak: The Church's Voice in Public Affairs.* Edinburgh: T & T Clark, 1995.

Clinebell, Howard. *Ecotherapy: Healing Ourselves, Healing the Earth.* New York: The Haworth Press, 1996.

Cobb, John. *Grace and Responsibility: A Wesleyan Theology for Today.* Nashville: Abingdon Press, 1995.

Cobb, John and Herman Daly. *For the Common Good: Redirecting the Economy Toward Community, the Environment, and a Sustainable Future.* Boston: Beacon Press, 1989.

Cobb, John. *Sustainability: Economics, Ecology, and Justice.* Maryknoll: Orbis, 1992.

Cobb, John. *Earthist Challenge to Economism: A Theological Critique of the World Bank.* New York: St. Martin's Press, 1999.

Coles, Robert. *The Spiritual Life of Children.* Boston: Houghton Mifflin, 1990.

____. *Migrants, Sharecroppers, Mountaineers.* Boston: Little, Brown, 1971.

____. *Eskimos, Chicanos, Indians.* Boston: Little, Brown, 1971.

____. *The Moral Life of Children.* Boston: Atlantic Monthly Press, 1986.

____. *The Political Life of Children.* Boston: Atlantic Monthly Press, 1986.

____. *In God's House: Children's Drawings.* Grand Rapids: Eerdmans, 1996.

____. *The Moral Intelligence of Children.* New York: Random House, 1997.

Collins, Kenneth J. *The Scripture Way of Salvation: The Heart of John Wesley's Theology.* Nashville: Abingdon Press, 1997.

Couture, Pamela. *Blessed Are the Poor? Women's Poverty, Family Policy, and Practical Theology.* Nashville: Abingdon Press, 1991.

Currie, Janet. *Welfare and the Well-being for Children.* Switzerland: Harwood Academic Publishers, 1995.

Daley, Shannon P. and Kathleen A. Guy. *Welcome the Child: A Child Advocacy Guide for Churches.* New York: Friendship Press and Children's Defense Fund, 1994.

David, Kenneth and Tony Charlton, eds. *Pastoral Care Matters in Primary and Middle Schools.* London: Routledge, 1996.

Dittes, James. *Driven by Hope: Men and Meaning.* Louisville: Westminster John Knox Press, 1996.

Douglas, J. D., gen. ed. *New Bible Dictionary.* Downers Grove: Intervarsity Press, 1996.

Drimmelen, Rob van. *Faith in a Global Economy: A Primer for Christians.* Geneva: WCC Publications, 1998.

Dufair, Xavier Lum, ed., *Dictionary of Bibical Theology.* 2nd ed. Translated from the French by P. Joseph Cahill, S.J. New York: Seabury Press, 1973.

Fiorenza, Elisabeth Schüssler, and Anne Carr, eds. *Women, Work, and Poverty: Concillium* 194. Edinburgh: T & T Clark, 1987.

Franklin, Robert M. *Another Day's Journey: Black Churches Confronting the American Crisis.* Minneapolis: Fortress Press, 1997.

Friedman, David Noel, ed. *The Anchor Bible Dictionary.* Anchor, New York: Doubleday, 1992.

Garbarino, James, Nancy Dubrow, Kathleen Kostelny, and Carole Pardo. *Children in Danger: Coping with the Consequences of Community Violence.* San Francisco: Jossey-Bass, 1992.

Garland, Diane. *Precious in His Sight: A Guide to Child Advocacy.* 2nd ed. Birmingham: New Hope, 1996.

Geertz, Clifford. *Interpretation of Cultures.* New York: BasicBooks, 1973.

Gerkin, Charles. *Introduction to Pastoral Care.* Nashville: Abingdon Press, 1997.

Gottmann, John Mordecai. *What Predicts Divorce? The Relationship Between Marital Processes and Marital Outcomes.* Lawrence Erlbaum Assoc., 1994.

Gottmann, John Mordecai, with Nan Silver. *Why Marriages Succeed and Fail: And How You Can Make Yours Last.* New York: Fireside, 1995.

Goudzwaard, Bob and Harry de Lange. *Beyond Poverty and Affluence: Toward an Economy of Care with a Twelve Step Program for Economic Recovery.* Translated into English and edited by Mark R. Van der Vennen. Grand Rapids: Eerdmans, 1995.

Greenspahn, Frederick E. *When Brothers Dwell Together: The Preeminence of Younger Siblings in the Hebrew Bible.* New York: Oxford University Press, 1994.

Harrington, Michael. *The New American Poverty.* New York: Penguin Books, 1984.

Hastings, James. *A Dictionary of the Bible.* Peabody, Massachusetts: Hendrickson Publishers, 1988.

Heilbroner, Robert. *Behind the Veil of Economics.* New York: W. W. Norton, 1989.

Herzog, William R. *Parables as Subversive Speech: Jesus as the Pedagogue of the Oppressed.* Louisville: Westminster John Knox Press, 1994.

Hunt, Richard A., Rita Demaria, Larry Hof. *Marriage Enrichment: Preparation, Mentoring, and Outreach.* Philadelphia: Brunner-Mazel, 1998.

Jewett, Robert. *Romans.* Nashville: Graded Press, 1988.

Junker-Kenny, Maureen, and Norbert Mette, eds. *Little Children Suffer: Concilium 2.* Maryknoll: Orbis, 1996.

Karoly, Lynn A., Peter W. Greenwood, Susan S. Everingham, Jill Haube, M. Rebecca Kilbourn, C. Peter Rydell, Matthew Sanders, and James Chiesa. *Investing in Our Children: What We Know and Don't Know About the Costs and Benefits of Early Childhood Interventions.* Santa Monica, Calif.: Rand, 1998.

Key, Ellen. *Century of the Child.* New York: G. P. Putnam's Sons, 1909.

Kilbourn, Phyllis, ed. Street Children: *A Guide to Effective Ministry.* Monrovia, Calif.: MARC, 1997.

_____. *Children in Crisis: A New Commitment.* Monrovia, Calif.: MARC, 1997.

_____. *Healing the Children of War.* Monrovia, Calif.: MARC, 1995.

Kornfeld, Margaret Zipse. *Cultivating Wholeness: A Guide to Care and Counseling in Faith Communities.* New York: Continuum, 1998.

Kotlowitz, Alex. *There Are No Children Here: The Story of Two Boys Growing Up in the Other America.* New York: Anchor Books, 1992.

Kozol, Jonathan. *Amazing Grace: The Lives of Children and the Conscience of a Nation.* New York: HarperCollins, 1996.

Kretzmann, John P. and John L. McKnight. *Building Communities from the Inside Out: A Path Toward Finding and Mobilizing a Community's Assets.* Evanston: Northwestern University Center for Urban Affairs and Policy Research, 1993.

Lartey, Emmanuel Y. *In Living Colour: An Intercultural Approach to Pastoral Care and Counselling.* London: Cassel, 1997.

Lefkowitz, Rochelle, and Ann Whithorn. *For Crying Out Loud: Women and Poverty in the United States.* New York: Pilgrim Press, 1986.

Lerner, Gerda. *Black Women in White America: A Documentary History.* New York: Vintage, 1973.

Lester, Andrew. *Hope in Pastoral Care and Counseling.* Louisville: Westminster John Knox Press, 1995.

_____. *Pastoral Care with Children in Crisis.* Philadelphia: Westminster, 1985.

_____. ed. *When Children Suffer: A Sourcebook for Ministry with Children in Crisis.* Philadelphia: Westminster, 1987.

Louv, Richard. *Children's Future.* New York: Anchor Books, 1992.

Lum, Doman. *Social Work Practice and People of Color: A Process-Stage Approach.* Belmont, Calif.: Brooks-Cole Publishing Company, 1986.

Maddox, Randy. *Responsible Grace: John Wesley's Practical Theology.* Nashville: Kingswood Books, 1994.

Males, Mike A. *Framing Youth: Ten Myths About the Next Generation.* Monroe, Maine: Common Courage Press, 1999.

Meeks, Douglas. *God the Economist: The Doctrine of God and Political Economy.* Minneapolis: Fortress Press, 1989.

Miller, Madeline S., ed., and J. Lane Miller. *Harper's Bible Dictionary.* New York: Harper & Row, 1973.

Miller-McLemore, Bonnie. *Also a Mother: Work and Family as a Theological Dilemma.* Nashville: Abingdon Press, 1994.

Mills, Watson E. gen.ed. *Mercer Dictionary of the Bible.* Macon, Georgia: Mercer University Press, 1990.

Moore, Mary Elizabeth. *Ministering with the Earth.* St. Louis: Chalice Press, 1998.

Myers, Barbara Kimes, and William R. Myers. *Engaging in Transcendence: The Church's Ministry and Covenant with Young Children.* Cleveland: Pilgrim Press, 1992.

Neuger, Christie Cozad and James Newton Poling. *The Care of Men.* Nashville: Abingdon Press, 1997.

Newsom, Carol A. and Sharon Ringe, eds. *The Women's Bible Commentary.* Louisville: Westminster John Knox Press, 1992.

Nyala, Hannah. *Point Last Seen: A Woman Tracker's Story.* Boston: Beacon Press, 1997.

O'Brien, Timothy L. *Bad Bet: The Inside Story of the Glamour, Glitz, and Danger of America's Gambling Industry.* New York: Random House/Times Business, 1998.

Outler, Albert Cook. *The Wesleyan Theological Heritage: Essays of Albert C. Outler.* Grand Rapids: Zondervan, 1991.

Pais, Janet. *Suffer the Children.* New York: Paulist, 1991.

Park, Andrew Sung. *The Wounded Heart of God: The Asian Concept of Han and the Christian Doctrine of Sin.* Nashville: Abingdon Press, 1993.

Pattison, Stephen with James Woodward. *A Vision of Pastoral Theology: In Search of Words that Resurrect the Dead.* Contact Pastoral Monographs 4. Falkirk: United Kingdom, 1994.

Pecora, Peter J., James K. Whittaker, Anthony N. Maluccio, with Richard P. Barth and Robert D. Plotnick. *The Child Welfare Challenge: Policy, Practice, and Research.* New York: Aldine de Gruyter, 1992.

Peters, Ted, ed. "Children." *Dialog: A Journal of Theology,* 37:3 (summer 1998).

Petr, Christopher G. *Social Work with Children and Their Families: Pragmatic Foundations.* New York: Oxford University Press, 1998.

Ramshaw, Elaine. *Ritual and Pastoral Care.* Philadelphia: Fortress Press, 1987.

Richards, Laurence O. *A Theology of Children's Ministry.* Grand Rapids: Zondervan, 1983.

Runyon, Theodore. *The New Creation: John Wesley's Theology Today.* Nashville: Abingdon Press, 1998.

Runyon, Theodore, ed. *Sanctification and Liberation: Liberation Theology in Light of the Wesleyan Tradition.* Nashville: Abingdon, 1981.

Sherman, Arloc. *Wasting America's Future: The CDF Report on the Costs of Child Poverty.* Boston: Beacon Press, 1994.

Sidel, Ruth. *Women and Children Last: The Plight of Poor Women in Affluent America.* New York: Penguin Books, 1986.

Skocpol, Theda. *Protecting Mothers and Soldiers: The Political Origins of Social Policy in the United States.* Cambridge, Mass.: Belknap Press, 1992.

Sobrino, Jon. *The Principle of Mercy: Taking the Crucified People from the Cross.* Maryknoll: Orbis, 1994.

The State of America's Children: A Report from the Children's Defense Fund. Boston: Beacon Press, 1998.

Stegeman, W. *The Gospel and the Poor.* Translated by D. Elliott. Philadelphia: Fortress Press, 1984.

Tamez, Elsa. *Amnesty of Grace: Justification by Faith from a Latin American Perspective.* Translated by Sharon Ringe. Nashville: Abingdon Press, 1993.

Taylor, Michael. *Not Angels but Agencies: The Ecumenical Response to Poverty—A Primer.* Geneva: WCC Publications, 1995.

Thompson, Tracey. *The Beast: A Reckoning with Depression.* New York: G. P. Putnam's Sons, 1995.

Treat, James. *Native and Christian: Indigenous Voices on Religious Identity in the United States and Canada.* New York: Routledge, 1996.

Trimiew, Darryl M. *Voices of the Silenced: The Responsible Self in a Marginalized Community.* Cleveland: Pilgrim Press, 1993.

Underwood, Ralph. *Pastoral Care and the Means of Grace.* Minneapolis: Augsburg Fortress, 1993.

Weaver, Jace, ed. *Defending Mother Earth: Native American Perspectives on Environmental Justice.* Maryknoll: Orbis, 1996.

Weber, Max. *The Sociology of Religion.* Translated by Ephriam Fischoff. First published in Germany, J.C.B. Mohr, 1922. Boston: Beacon Press, 1963.

Weitzman, Lenore. *The Divorce Revolution: The Unexpected Social and Economic Consequences for Women and Children in the United States.* New York: The Free Press, 1985.

Wesley, John. *The Works of John Wesley.* Vols. 1-4. Oxford: Oxford University Press, 1975.

Wheeler, Sondra Ely. *Wealth as Peril and Obligation: The New Testament on Possessions.* Grand Rapids: Eerdmans, 1995.

Williams, Constance Willard. *Black Teenage Mothers: Pregnancy and Child Rearing from Their Perspective.* Lexington: Lexington Books, 1991.

Williams, Delores S. *Sisters in the Wilderness: The Challenge of Womanist God-Talk.* Maryknoll: Orbis, 1993.

Wilson, William Julius. *The Truly Disadvantaged: The Inner City, the Underclass, and Public Policy.* Chicago: University of Chicago Press, 1987.

Wolfe, Alan. *Whose Keeper? Social Science and Moral Obligation.* Berkeley, Calif.: University of California Press, 1989.

Zigler, Edward F., Sharon Lynn Kagan, and Nancy W. Hall. *Children, Families, and Government: Preparing for the Twenty First Century.* Cambridge: Cambridge University Press, 1996.

DENOMINATIONAL MATERIALS

"All God's Children? Children's Evangelism in Crisis: A Report from the General Synod Board of Education and Board of Mission. London: National Society/Church House Publishing, 1991.

Children and Families First: Campaign. Parish Resource Manual. U.S. Catholic Conference of Bishops. Washington D.C., 1992. (Roman Catholic)

"Ihnen Gehört das Reich Gottes—Kinder und Armut als Herausforderung für die Kirche," Evangelisch-methodischen Kirche in Deutschland, Stuttgart: Druckhaus West. (Methodist)

See "Resource Catalog" for the United Methodist Episcopal Initiative on Children and Poverty, revised and distributed by the General Council on Ministries, Dayton, Ohio, April, 1999. For information contact "Shared Mission Focus on Young People Office," General Council on Ministries, 601 W. Riverview Ave., Dayton, Ohio 45406, telephone: 937-227-9400. Among those resources are listed:

"A Church for All God's Children," that can be downloaded from the Internet.

"Putting Children and their Families First: A Planning Handbook for Congregations," available from the General Board of Global Ministries service center.

"Safe Sanctuaries: Reducing the Risk of Child Abuse in the Church," available from the General Board of Discipleship, 1-800-685-4370.

ARTICLES

Augsburger, David, ed. "Multicultural Pastoral Care and Counseling." *Journal of Pastoral Care* 46 (summer 1992): 103-73.

Ballard, Paul, guest editor. "Partners in Concern." *Contact* 100 (1989).

Clinebell, Howard. "Looking Back, Looking Ahead: Toward an Ecological Systems Model for Pastoral Care and Counseling." *Journal of Pastoral Care* 46 (fall 1992): 263-72.

Couture, Pamela D. "The Context of Congregations: Pastoral Care in an Individualistic Context." In "Congregational Care." Edited by Carolyn Stahl Bohler and James N. Poling. *Journal of Pastoral Theology* 2 (summer 1992).

Couture, Pamela D. "Rethinking Public and Private Patriarchy." In *Religion, Feminism, and the Family.* Edited by Anne Carr and Mary Stewart van Leewen. Louisville: Westminster John Knox Press, 1996, 249-74.

Couture, Pamela D. "Revelation in Pastoral Theology: A Wesleyan Perspective." *Journal of Pastoral Theology* 2 (1999): 21-33.

Fensham, F. Charles. "The Widow, the Orphan, and the Poor in Ancient Near Eastern Legal and Wisdom Literature." *Journal of Near Eastern Studies* 21 (April 1962): 129-39.

Fowler, Gene. "Pastoral Care of the Congregation." *Journal of Pastoral Care* 51 (winter 1997): 377-94.

____. "Studying Pastoral Care in Congregations: A Hermeneutical Approach." *Journal of Pastoral Care* 52 (winter 1998): 323-38.

Gates, John. "Resilient Communities: The Power of Prevention." In *Strong Partners: Realigning Religious Health Assets for Community Health.* Atlanta: The Carter Center, 1997.

Gowan, Donald E. "Wealth and Poverty in the Old Testament: the Case of the Widow, the Orphan, and the Sojourner." *Interpretation* 41 (October 1987): 341-53.

Jennings, Theodore W. "Children and the Poor: Toward the Spiritual Renewal of the United Methodist Church." *Quarterly Review,* 17:4 (winter 1997–98): 311-33.

Justes, Emma. "Crossing Bridges of No Return." *Journal of Pastoral Theology* 6 (1996): 119-26.

Karaban, Roslyn A. "The Sharing of Cultural Variation." *Journal of Pastoral Care* 45 (spring 1991): 25-34.

Lartey, Emmanuel, guest editor. "Intercultural Issues in Pastoral Care" *Contact* 118 (1995).

Lyon, K. Brynolf. "What Is the Relevance of Congregational Studies for Pastoral Theology?" In "Congregational Care." Edited by Carolyn Stahl Bohler and James N. Poling. *Journal of Pastoral Theology* 2 (summer 1992).

Marshall, Joretta L. "Pastoral Care with Congregations in Social Stress." In Pamela D. Couture and Rodney J. Hunter. *Pastoral Care and Social Conflict: Essays in Honor of Charles V. Gerkin.* Nashville: Abingdon Press, 1995.

Orr, Judith L. "Theological Home and the Work of Neighbor Care (pastoral counseling with working-class women) *Journal of Pastoral Theology* 5 (1995): 28-37.

Outler, Albert C. "How to Run a Conservative Revolution and Get No Thanks for It." Presented to the John Wesley Theological Institute, Northern Illinois Conference of the United Methodist Church, February 11, 1986.

"Pastoral Care in Community." No guest editor. *Contact* 125 (1998).

Patterson, Richard D. "The Widow, the Orphan, and the Poor in the Old Testament and Extra-Biblical Literature." *Bibliotheca Sacra,* 130 (July 1973): 223-34.

Perkins-Buzo, J. Reid. "Theodicy in the Face of Children's Suffering and Death." *Journal of Pastoral Care* 48 (summer 1994): 155-61.

Roth, Kenneth, "Sidelined on Human Rights." *Foreign Affairs,* 77:2 (March/April, 1998): 2-7.

Schneider-Harpprecht, Christoph. "Family and Counseling in the Context of Poverty: Experiences from Brazil." *Journal of Pastoral Theology* 7 (1997): 129-48.

Spar, Debora L., "The Spotlight and the Bottom Line." *Foreign Affairs,* 77:2 (March/April, 1998): 7-13.

Voss, Richard W. "Pastoral Social Ministry in the Ecosystem of the Poor: Breaking Through the Illusions." *Journal of Pastoral Care* 47 (summer 1993): 100-08.

"America Answers Call to Help Kids." *Chronicle of Philanthropy,* April 23, 1998. http://philanthropy.com/articles.dir/i13.dir/13summit.htm.

"Faith Based Charities to the Rescue." *Chronicle of Philanthropy,* December 11, 1997. http://philanthropy.com/articles.dir/i13.dir.13summit.htm.

SELECTED INTERNET WEB SITES

http://hd.wsu.edu/publications/fathering/fathers.html.

Arloc Sherman, *Poverty Matters: The Cost of Child Poverty in America.* CDF, 1997. http://www.childrensdefense.org/fairstart_povmat.html.

The Institute for Research on Poverty at the University of Wisconsin has a directory of links at http://www.ssc.wisc.edu/irp/povlinks.htm.

Children, Youth and Family Consortium, University of Minnesota offers a comprehensive and annotated compilation of resources at http://www.cyfc.umn.edu/cyflinks.html# youth.

The National Center for Children and Poverty at Columbia University is located at http://cpmcnet.columbia.edu/dept/nccp/.

The Joint Center for Poverty Research at the University of Chicago and Northwestern University provides its working papers at http://www.jcpr.org/wpseries.html#sufficient.

An Annotated Bibliography on Homeless Families and Children, compiled in June 1997, was prepared for the National Resource Center on Homelessness and Mental Illness, Policy Research Associates, Inc., under contract number 278-91-0016 with the Center for Mental Health Services (CMHS), Substance Abuse and Mental Health Services Administration, U.S. Department of Health and Human Services, Rockville, Maryland: http://www.prainc.com/nrc/bibliographies/fam_child.htm.

UNICEF materials can be downloaded from the UNICEF website, http://www.unicef.org.

The entire United Nations Convention on the Rights of the Child can be found on the Internet at http://www.freethechildren.org/uncrcdoc.htm. A summary may be found at http://www.unicef.org/crc/coven.htm.

Annie Casey Foundation Kids Count: www.aecf.org/kidscount.kc1999/.

INDEX